TIME-CONSTRAINED EVALUATION

EDUCATIONAL MANAGEMENT SERIES
Edited by Cyril Poster

TIME-CONSTRAINED EVALUATION

A practical approach for LEAs and schools

Brian Wilcox

London and New York

First published 1992
by Routledge
11 New Fetter Lane, London EC4P 4EE

Simultaneously published in the USA and Canada
by Routledge
a division of Routledge, Chapman and Hall, Inc.
29 West 35th Street, New York, NY 10001

Typeset in Palatino by
Falcon Typographic Art Ltd,
Edinburgh & London
Printed and bound in Great Britain by Biddles Ltd,
Guildford and King's Lynn

British Library Cataloguing in Publication Data
Wilcox, B. (Brian)
Time-constrained evaluation: a practical approach
for LEA's and schools. – (Educational management
series)
I. Title   II. Series
379.15
0–415–06968–8
0–415–06969–6

Library of Congress Cataloging in Publication Data
is available

CONTENTS

FIGURES

FOREWORD

Nobody involved in education, whether in schools and colleges, in LEAs or in national, regional or local projects, questions the need for evaluation. The problem has always been twofold: to find the time for it and to command the skills necessary for a process that will have external validity.

This book provides a solution to both aspects of the problem. Recognising that time is a concern, even more in recent years than ever before, it offers processes that are time-constrained: processes, that is, that accept this resource limitation and work within it. Among these processes, self-evaluation is given a high profile. This is important, since evaluation will increasingly have to be undertaken at the point of impact, with LEA inspectors and advisers validating the process.

Because evaluation has in the past been undertaken mainly either by independent consultants or by those in higher education acting in a consultancy role, there has grown up around it a certain mystique. Perhaps the most valuable contribution that Brian Wilcox's research project and this book will make is to demonstrate that the ability to mount an evaluation that has acceptable rigour lies within the capacity of middle and senior managers in educational establishments, TEED project managers, and LEA advisers and inspectors at all levels of seniority. It is a worthy addition to the Routledge Education Management series.

Cyril Poster

PREFACE

Over the last twenty or more years there has grown up a substantial literature on educational evaluation. The fact remains, however, that this literature has had but modest effect on the practice of those in schools, colleges and LEAs. Although often invoked as an integral part of the educational process, evaluation has more often been honoured in the breach than in the observance.

An important aim of recent government policy has been to introduce more systematic approaches to evaluation in LEAs and their institutions. A similar intention is also apparent in the training field. For example, a major task of the new Technical and Enterprise Councils is to ensure that their programmes are subject to assessment within an overall evaluation strategy.

In the pages which follow, a conceptual framework is set out which unifies the separate traditions and approaches of inspection and evaluation theory with those of performance assessment and quality assurance. Within this framework are described methods and procedures which enable a variety of educational and training staff to organise and carry out realistic evaluations. Such staff include not only those in local and national inspectorates but also administrators, teachers and trainers.

The book addresses the fundamental problem of how to ensure that evaluations can be carried out in short periods of time so as to provide useful and trustworthy information to those responsible for managing educational institutions and programmes.

The approach outlined is based on the findings of the Training

Agency funded project *Inspection Methodologies for Education and Training* (IMET) which was carried out by the author between January 1989 and October 1990. The book is adapted from the project report, which is Crown copyright, by permission of the Controller of HMSO.

LIST OF ABBREVIATIONS USED

ALIS	A-Level Information System
ATO	Approved Training Organisation
BS	British Standard
BSI	British Standards Institution
CEO	Chief Education Officer
CI	Chief Inspector
DES	Department of Education and Science
ERA	Education Reform Act (1988)
ESG	Education Support Grant
ET	Employment Training
GCSE	General Certificate of Secondary Education
HDP	Hermeneutic Dialectic Process
HMI	Her Majesty's Inspectorate
HM Inspectors	Her Majesty's Inspectors
ILEA	Inner London Education Authority
LAPP	Lower Attaining Pupils Programme
LEA	Local Education Authority
LMS	Local Management of Schools
MSC	Manpower Services Commission, subsequently retitled the Training Agency (TA) and now known as the Training, Enterprise and Education Directorate (TEED) of the Department of Employment
NFER	National Foundation for Educational Research
NGT	Nominal Group Technique
PI	Performance Indicator

QA	Quality Assurance
QC	Quality Control
RE	Religious Education
RI	Reporting Inspector
SAT	Standardised Assessment Task
SCI	Senior Chief Inspector
SCRE	Scottish Council for Research in Education
SI	Staff Inspector
TA	Training Agency (see also MSC)
TCE	Time-Constrained Evaluation
TEC	Technical and Enterprise Council
TEED	Training, Enterprise and Education Directorate (see also MSC)
TSAS	Training Standards Advisory Service
TSI	Training Standards Inspector
TVEI	Technical Vocational Education Initiative
TVEE	Technical Vocational Education Extension
YT	Youth Training, formerly Youth Training Scheme (YTS)

1

EVALUATION: AN OVERVIEW

THE CURRENT CONTEXT

Throughout the 1980s the education service was subjected to a plethora of government initiatives intended to promote major changes in schools and colleges and thereby in the learning opportunities of pupils and students. The momentum of change increased with the arrival of the Education Reform Act (HMSO, 1988). This ushered in a period of major upheaval in which the assumptions, structures and practices underpinning the public education system since the Butler Act of 1944 are being fundamentally transformed. This climate of change has not been confined to education. The provision of training has undergone remarkable development particularly as a consequence of the activities of the Manpower Services Commission since its creation in the mid-1970s. The MSC, in 1988 renamed the Training Agency and in 1990 reformed as the Training, Enterprise and Education Directorate of the Department of Employment, has been responsible for a number of national programmes and initiatives to improve preparation for work and vocational training.

Education and training are at the top of the political agenda of governments in most countries irrespective of their particular ideology. Why is this? A major reason lies in the belief that education and training are necessary conditions for a country's economic and technological growth and consequently for achieving high living standards for its citizens. A second reason is that education and training make a very substantial call on the public purse. It is therefore necessary to ensure that money is wisely spent, that what is achieved is relevant

1

to the economic and other aspirations of government and that the standards attained are the highest possible.

The third reason relates to the special function which education has in the modern secular state. Because of its compulsory nature and the broadening of its remit beyond that of narrow 'schooling', the education system now acts as the only guaranteed means for inducting the young systematically into the worlds of skills, ideas and values. It is the curriculum in particular which is crucial to that induction process.

A curriculum is no less than the knowledge system of society, and therefore not only an ontology but also the metaphysics and ideology which that society has agreed to recognise as legitimate and truthful; it sets the canons of truthfulness.

(Inglis, 1985: 22–3)

The induction role that was played in former times by the family, the church and the local community is now much less influential and extends to only a proportion of youth. While the media and the closely related manifestations of youth culture undoubtedly have an effect, their educative function is incidental and unsystematic. The education system, alone among all other influences and agencies, provides a programme available to all which has as its central concern the development of individuals as rational and moral beings. The education system, despite its inadequacies, has as its ultimate purpose the transformation of individuals and society. Training schemes, particularly for the young, with their frequent espousal of the importance of personal and social development as well as of the specifically vocational, share some of these broader aspirations of education.

For these reasons it is important that knowledge of the quality and effects of education and training is widely available. This should be a major concern at all times even when education and training systems are stable and in equilibrium with society at large. It is even more the case at a time, like the present, of radical change. Those responsible for providing education and training at whatever level – class or group, school, college or training centre, locally or nationally – should ensure that information is regularly available on what is offered. Such information is clearly necessary if administrators, teachers,

2

trainers and others are to carry out their responsibilities effectively and imaginatively. It is also important that information is made available to parents, employers and the community at large. For knowledge about education and training is a proper concern of an informed citizenry.

All that has been said so far has been to reinforce the central role that *evaluation* should play in the provision of education and training. For the knowledge needed is not simply descriptive. It should also be evaluative, that is, indicating something of the quality or merit of the aspects of education and training which it depicts. Evaluation and the closely related notion of *accountability* have been persistent themes in national educational policies of recent years. Both have been expressions of the growing disquiet about the standards of the public education system felt by successive governments over the last decade and a half. A concern for standards in a climate of financial cut-backs to education has inevitably given evaluation a sense of political importance and urgency. The emphasis on evaluation has been particularly focused on the need to assess the performance of schools. In 1977 LEAs were reminded of the necessity to evaluate schools.

> Local education authorities need to be able to assess the relative performance of their schools to reach decisions about staffing, the allocation of resources, and other matters. In particular, it is an essential facet of their accountability for educational standards that they must be able to identify schools which consistently perform poorly, so that appropriate remedial action can be taken.
>
> (HMSO, 1977: para 3.7)

It was assumed that this task would be carried out by LEA advisers:

> They provide well developed methods of describing and assessing the system and the institutions within it, the evidence they gather contributes to the support and development of schools, and points to any remedial action if a school is consistently less than satisfactory.
>
> (HMSO, 1977: para 3.4)

By the mid-1980s concern about the standards of schools and

3

the variability of provision within them was unambiguously addressed in the government white paper *Better Schools*.

> The Government believes that, not least in the light of what is being achieved in other countries, the standards now generally attained by our pupils are neither as good as they can be, nor as good as they need to be if young people are equipped for the world of the twenty first century . . . . The present spectrum of quality and the variations between schools are wider than is acceptable in a national system of school education based on 11 years of compulsory attendance.
>
> (HMSO, 1984: paras 9 and 16)

Again the importance of LEAs assessing the quality of their provision was stressed:

> Within each LEA, important functions are exercised, under the direction of the CEO, by local advisers (sometimes called inspectors). They play a central role in reporting to the authority, on the basis of visits and inspections, on the quality of education being provided in its schools.
>
> (HMSO, 1984: para 266)

Despite the emphasis given to the importance of the evaluation function of LEAs in successive government and DES reports, there was little evidence of its systematic development in the majority of LEAs. Studies of advisers have shown that they carry out a multitude of functions of which inspection and other forms of evaluation may be very much a minority activity. Indeed many advisers appear not to see inspection and evaluation as part of their job and are ambivalent about it (Bolam *et al.*, 1978). The most recent study, carried out in 1986–7 (Stillman, 1988; Stillman and Grant, 1989), indicates that on average advisers spend less than 10 per cent of their time on formal inspections. Moreover there appears to be such a bewildering array of different approaches as to indicate considerable conceptual and methodological confusion about the nature and practice of evaluation.

The situation is, however, changing rapidly as a consequence of the Education Reform Act (ERA). ERA is a powerful

4

embodiment of the government's commitment to standards, freedom and choice in education. These implicitly underwrite the importance of evaluation as a means of providing information about schools, not least to help consumers in their choice of school and educational opportunities generally. Kenneth Baker, the then Secretary of State, and the DES were at pains to emphasise the crucial role in the evaluation of schools of LEA advisers, increasingly referred to as local inspectors.

> The local inspectorates will need to monitor and evaluate school performance. They will need to provide LEAs and the schools themselves with trusted and informed professional advice, based on first hand observation of what schools are actually doing, of the way they are implementing the national curriculum, and of the standards achieved.
>
> (Baker, 1988: para 10)

Evaluation will be particularly linked to the introduction of schemes of local management of schools which involve formula funding and the delegation of financial and managerial responsibilities to governing bodies.

> LEAs should aim to generate as part of their monitoring cycle appropriate data with which to evaluate the success of their schemes. This evaluation should serve two purposes. First, LEAs will need to assess their success in implementing their schemes in the initial period . . . . Secondly, LEAs will need to evaluate on an on-going basis the success of local management in improving the quality of teaching and learning in their schools.
>
> (DES, 1988a: para 155)

Financial support has been made available to LEAs in a five-year programme from 1989–90 under the Education Support Grant (ESG) arrangements to help them develop coherent inspection policies and to appoint extra advisers (DES, 1988b). It is apparent from advertisements and articles which have appeared in the educational press since the Act that the title of inspector is becoming more common and that an increasing number of LEAs are developing inspectorates as key components of new, reorganised education departments.

A not dissimilar situation is apparent in the field of training. In recent years the MSC vigorously promoted the cause of evaluation as a key requirement in implementing the range of training programmes which it created. For example, the Technical Vocational Education Initiative (TVEI) has a substantial network of national and local evaluation activities associated with it. Evaluation in the form of a *programme review* is a required feature for the approval of a Youth Training (YT) scheme. Managing agents of schemes are encouraged to review progress by, for example, gathering information on trainee destinations after training, trainee views on certain elements of training and employer views on the relevance of training (MSC, 1986). Schemes are also subject to inspection by the Training Standards Advisory Service (TSAS), a national inspectorate established in 1986, which also now has a remit to inspect Employment Training (ET) schemes.

Training and Enterprise Councils (TECs) have been established to take over YT and other programmes formerly the responsibility of the Training Agency (TA). In most instances the TECs will not operate schemes and programmes directly but will contract for their provision through a variety of agencies. A major task of the TECs will be to ensure that training programmes are subject to proper oversight. TECs then, rather like LEAs, will need to develop substantial evaluation programmes.

The questions which policy makers ask about the efficiency and effectiveness of education and training provision require answers which are frequently neither simple nor self-evident. It is regrettable that the public debate often fails to recognise the complexity of the issues involved and is frequently conducted in strident and trivial terms. The proper study of evaluation by policy makers and practitioners alike is essential if informed judgement, rather than individual prejudice, is to be brought to bear on these important matters.

EVALUATION, MONITORING, INSPECTION

Evaluation is a somewhat vague concept for many educationists. It is frequently linked with monitoring and inspection, terms which are themselves seldom defined. Much confusion and uncertainty surrounds their use. A general clarification is therefore necessary before the argument on which this book rests can be advanced.

Beeby (1977) offers one of the best of many definitions of evaluation:

> the systematic collection and interpretation of evidence leading, as part of the process, to a judgement of value with a view to action.
>
> (Quoted in Wolf, 1987: 8)

This definition succinctly incorporates four important attributes.

- Evaluation is based on evidence which is *systematically* collected.
- The meaning of evidence is seldom unambiguous and therefore needs to be *interpreted*.
- *Judgements of value* are made about the entity being evaluated and its effects.
- Evaluation is *action oriented*, intended to lead to better practices and policies.

Not all evaluators would agree with this definition. Some would reject the judgemental nature of evaluation. For example, Cronbach *et al.* (1980) advocate an approach that perceives the evaluator as:

> an educator [whose] success is to be judged by what others learn . . . rather than a referee . . . who is hired to decide who is 'right' or 'wrong'.
>
> (Quoted in Nevo, 1986: 17)

Beeby's definition can apply to the evaluation of any entity: individual, programme or institution. We shall not be concerned here with the first of these. Where evaluation is concerned with specific individuals the term assessment is usually employed in the case of students and trainees and appraisal for teachers and lecturers. The focus of the book will be on the evaluation of educational institutions and programmes. It is, of course, true to say that the evaluation of these may nevertheless involve assessment of pupils or teachers: for example, by testing the former or interviewing the latter. The purpose, however, is not to generate information about the individual *qua* individual but to aggregate the data from individuals in order to understand better some aspects of the institution or programme in which they are involved.

The word monitoring is frequently used in conjunction with that of evaluation although it seems to lack an agreed definition. For example, the term is not listed in the British Educational Thesaurus (Marder and Johnson, 1988). Monitoring is perhaps more familiar in non-educational contexts. The progress towards building a house is monitored by site visits to note the stages of construction against previously agreed plans and specifications. The financial soundness of an organisation is monitored through the standard procedures of audit. These examples suggest that the general process of monitoring involves the collection of information, on a regular basis, in order to check on the progress of an activity or the state of a system. The intention is that significant departures from the expected should lead to appropriate corrective action.

The implication is that monitoring relies upon the identification of indicators which can be reliably assessed against predetermined standards or targets. The more indicators which are used, the greater will be the amount of available information about the entity being monitored. The information may be capable of an interpretation which is essentially evaluative or it may prompt additional activity and the collection of further information which makes a subsequent evaluation possible. In other words, monitoring is an on-going process carried out on a system in order to yield regular information about aspects of its condition or level of functioning. Each element of monitoring information is evaluative in the sense that reaching or exceeding the target or standard is considered to be better than falling below it. The more the individual items of monitored information can be interpreted and aggregated to give a comprehensive description of the quality and effectiveness of the system, the more monitoring can be said to shade into evaluation.

Evaluations are often conceived of as discrete, one-off exercises. Indeed much of the literature on evaluation derives from such exercises. While there is clearly a need for specific evaluations in LEAs and TECs, the linking of monitoring and evaluation implies that an on-going process of evaluation, deriving from regular monitoring, will be a major means of assessing institutions and programmes. In education the government envisages that such monitoring and evaluation will be a principal responsibility of LEA advisers.

Inspection is an example of a method of evaluation which is surprisingly poorly documented. There are probably several reasons for this neglect. Much of the writing on evaluation comes from the USA where inspection is not a feature of the public education system. Evaluation there is largely conducted by external evaluators appointed to funded programmes. Another reason may be that the main contributors to evaluation theory and methodology, including those in Britain, have been academics and educational researchers. They may not therefore have recognised the work of inspectors as falling within what they understand as the legitimate parameters of evaluation. A further reason is that the outcomes of inspection, in the form of reports by Her Majesty's Inspectorate (HMI), have become publicly available only since 1983 and thereby open to scrutiny (Gray and Hannon, 1986; Elliott and Ebbutt, 1986). Inspection, then, has tended to be a somewhat shadowy and ill-understood approach to the monitoring and evaluation of the public education system. This is particularly regrettable since it is arguable that much of what is known about education in the public domain has been influenced more by the findings of HMI than by those of researchers and professional evaluators.

LEAs are faced with the task of organising programmes through which their education provision can be monitored and evaluated on a regular basis. Ideally such programmes should include all LEA institutions, services, programmes and projects. A comparable challenge will face the TECs in relationship to the multitude of training schemes within their remit. The literature of educational evaluation, although very substantial, has tended not to concentrate on this kind of situation. The literature is mainly concerned with the evaluations of discrete, one-off entities, frequently in the form of innovative curriculum projects. Although LEAs and TECs are clearly interested in the evaluation of innovations much of their effort will be devoted to the evaluation of existing programmes and schemes. Furthermore, because of the central role which institutions play in the delivery of educational and training services, LEAs will be particularly concerned with monitoring and evaluating schools and colleges. This is an issue to which the conventional literature of evaluation has given scant attention.

Those concerned with system-wide evaluation inevitably face a major dilemma: the range of institutions and programmes to be evaluated far outstrips the level of resources which can realistically be given to that task. This leads to the necessity not only of defining priorities for evaluation but also of devising means of carrying out evaluations within periods of time significantly shorter than those customarily described as exemplary in the textbooks and journals of evaluation.

JUSTIFICATION OF EVALUATION

There are two major functions which evaluation is often said to serve:

- aiding decision makers in the tasks of improvement;
- demonstrating accountability.

Both of these functions are apparent in the evaluation activities of LEAs. For example, if the planning and management of education are to be conducted efficiently and effectively it is necessary that decision makers have access to up-to-date, reliable and relevant information. Evaluation should make an important contribution to the information base available to LEAs and their institutions. Much of the justification for evaluation must rest upon its demonstrable usefulness to managers. The evaluation of an institution or programme should provide information which:

- identifies weaknesses to be remedied;
- identifies strengths and achievements which might be disseminated to others;
- facilitates the formulation of strategies for further development.

In other words, information from evaluation should help those in the LEA and its schools and colleges to devise the various programmes of support necessary for the maintainance and development of the education service.

In the life of actual institutions and programmes there may be relatively few discrete moments when the results of evaluation are available to inform specific actions. It is therefore better to conceive of evaluation and action as parts of an interactive process. This means that evaluation should be built in as an on-going process rather than being a one-off and relatively rare special event. Such a process would ensure that information is continuously generated to form a dynamic knowledge base available to decision makers. It is clearly impossible to develop a knowledge base sufficiently comprehensive to provide relevant information on every possible aspect at all times. Rather the aim should be to ensure that at any point in time something is known about the general state of an institution, programme, LEA or TEC and that more detailed knowledge is available on some specific aspects. The nature of these specific aspects might be expected to vary from time to time according to current interests and priorities.

The emphasis on monitoring and evaluation – particularly through inspection – is an expression of the government's concern to increase the public accountability of schools. There are several problems in making this intention a reality. First, the government assumes that the criteria for defining educational performance and the methodology for determining the extent to which individual schools meet them are unproblematic. For the government the task is essentially one of defining the outcomes of education and assessing their achievement by individual schools using inspection in all its forms. The fact is, however, that there is a general lack of consensus on both issues. Outcome measures, even those as apparently straightforward as examination results, do not speak for themselves. Their relationship to assumed input and process factors is complex and even the use of advanced statistical techniques has had only limited success in clarifying its nature. Inspection, despite its long history in the British education system, remains surprisingly obscure as a methodology of evaluation, at least to those other than inspectors.

The second problem is concerned with the issue of accountability for the performance of schools. Much of the relevant literature tends to focus on the accountability of individuals (Becher *et al.*, 1978; Elliott, 1980; Kogan, 1986). Thus, where accountability can be individually assigned it may be defined as:

a condition in which individual role holders are liable to review and the application of sanctions if their actions fail to satisfy those with whom they are in an accountable relationship.

(Kogan, 1986: 25)

It might be thought that in the case of schools it is headteachers who are accountable for performance. This assumes, however, that headteachers have total control over the many individuals and activities that contribute to the functioning of the school. This is clearly not the case. Moreover, there will be other factors over which the headteachers will have little or no influence, for example the level of resourcing and condition of the buildings. Is it therefore realistic to hold the headteacher to account for overall performance? If not, can specific accountabilities be assigned to the headteacher and individual members of staff? This is typically done in the formulation of job specifications and may be formally assessed in schemes of teacher appraisal. It is difficult to see, however, how such specific accountabilities can be related to the kind of global outcomes in which school performance might be expressed. In reality an individual teacher is not 'an Island entire of itself' but a member of a complex interactive whole. Consequently it is difficult to single out the unique contribution which an individual makes to the general performance of a school. Individual accountability therefore has to give way to the less precise notion of collective acountability.

The third problem in defining the accountabilities of schools is to clarify to whom accountability is due. The situation is again complex. Accountability is not to a single agency but to several. Schools are accountable to the LEA and increasingly to their governors. In addition accountability extends to parents, the local community and the public in general.

This raises some fundamental questions about what information should be made available to whom. For example, do governors and parents have the right to know the full extent of information which is available on a school, including evaluations by local inspectors? Some restrictions on the free availability of information seem to be envisaged:

> I do not mean that all inspectors' findings should be made available to everyone. But where a summary or selection

of findings can be made available this should promote the accountability of schools to the community and the community's interest in local institutions.

(Chamier, 1989)

Deciding what information should be available to the public and in what form is a contentious issue. LEAs will need to draw up a set of principles to guide practice in this area.

EXTERNAL AND INTERNAL EVALUATION

Inspection is an example of *external evaluation*, where the assessment of institutions or programmes is carried out by those who are not part of them. In the past schools and colleges have probably been more familiar with external evaluation by HMI than by local inspectors. HMI carries out an annual inspection programme involving samples of all types of educational institution. A range of inspection approaches is adopted of which perhaps the most familiar is the full inspection of a school or college. All major inspections involve the production of a report to the institution and LEA concerned, which, since 1983, is also available to the public. Short inspection visits are also carried out by inspectors, individually or in groups, and often limited to a single day. No formal report is issued. Nevertheless, these visits contribute to HMI's knowledge of the education system and its publications on provision.

Inspection by HMI ensures that educational standards and trends are assessed in order that the Secretary of State is regularly advised on the performance of the education service nationally. In addition, since many HMI reports describe individual institutions and programmes, they also contribute to the knowledge of provision in those specific localities in which they are situated. HMI reports contribute, then, not only to a national programme of evaluation but to local programmes as well. As a result they may be significant in matters of local accountability. For example, an HMI report on an individual school provides evidence for those to whom the head is accountable: the governors, the LEA and, perhaps more distantly, the DES. The school itself is not accountable to HMI. HMI may not instruct the headteacher to carry out some course of action; it does, however, identify those aspects of the school which require

13

attention. At local level HMI is an agency through which the accountability of those in educational institutions is expressed to those who have the power to enforce.

Apart from inspection by local and HM inspectors, LEAs have become accustomed to another form of external evaluation associated with the introduction in the early 1980s of *categorical funding*. Categorical funding involves LEAs in bidding for funds from the DES, TA and similar bodies, in order to support curriculum and other initiatives which are determined nationally. The funding is subject to a number of strings and is for a predetermined time (Harland, 1987). One of the strings is the requirement that an evaluation of the initiative must be carried out. TVEI provides the paradigm example of categorical funding. Other initiatives which have been implemented in this way include the Lower Attaining Pupils Programme (LAPP) and Educational Support Grants (ESGs) dealing with a range of projects covering the primary, secondary and post-16 sectors. These projects within individual LEAs have been evaluated locally by a variety of external evaluators many of whom will nevertheless have come from within the locality. They included teachers seconded part-time or full-time and academics from education departments in institutions of higher education. In addition, in the case of TVEI and LAPP, full-time teams were recruited to evaluate a national sample of the projects.

Evaluators may be regarded as a special kind of educational researcher. At any one time most LEAs will be hosts to educational researchers. These may be working within an LEA and its institutions as part of a national or regional sample. Other researchers may be local teachers working on projects within their own schools or carrying out investigations as thesis topics for a higher degree. An individual piece of research will, of course, have its own specific objectives which may not necessarily be directly connected with evaluation. However, where research is being carried out for whatever reason, feedback on the findings may provide some information which incidentally serves an evaluative purpose. It therefore behoves those in an institution where research is under way to keep themselves as fully informed about its progress and outcomes as is possible and appropriate.

Internal evaluation occurs when an institution or programme is assessed by those who are participants within it rather than

14

by outsiders. Internal evaluation is also sometimes known as *self-evaluation*, or *institution-based self-evaluation*. Where a school is involved the term *school self-evaluation* is used.

In the late 1970s and early 1980s a number of LEAs espoused the cause of self-evaluation as an alternative to inspection. They either sought to implement LEA-wide schemes or encouraged their schools to devise their own. The general effect of this initiative was disappointing (see Clift *et al.*, 1987). Although in some cases school self-evaluation, perhaps better termed *school-based review*, was influential in carrying through programmes of change it did not take hold in the vast majority of schools and seldom, if ever, functioned as an appropriate instrument of accountability. There are, however, several reasons why self-evaluation may be more successful in the new climate engendered by the ERA. First, the local management of schools (LMS) requires an annual review by schools of their performance as a key process in the setting of an annual budget. In other words a major part of the ERA apparatus, LMS, makes it certain that performance will need to be reviewed in some way.

Another relevant requirement of schools is that they should formulate annual curriculum plans setting out how they intend to implement the National Curriculum (DES, 1989a). Some schools have extended this notion to a general development plan embracing all the main aspects of a school's concerns. A recent project (Hargreaves *et al.*, 1989) has outlined a rationale and methodology for school development plans which is likely to be influential. A developmental cycle is envisaged involving the implementation of a plan which concentrates on three or four major priorities. Plans will be constructed in detail for the year ahead with longer-term priorities for the following two to three years described in outline only. The merit of the proposals is that they focus self-evaluation on to very specific priorities and targets. The approach is therefore likely to overcome both the unrealistic comprehensiveness and general vagueness of purpose which characterised some of the earlier efforts in self-evaluation.

External evaluation of institutions by inspection or self-evaluation tends to rely heavily on the use of qualitative judgements. The recent emphasis given to the assessment of performance has prompted renewed interest in the search for more quantitative and 'objective' measures of the achievements of institutions and programmes. Much of this has been concerned with the creation of appropriate *performance indicators* (PIs). Despite the growing attention paid to performance indicators they lack a broadly agreed definition. For the time being it will be sufficient to note that the term conveys an emphasis both on performance, as distinct from intention, and on indicators, as something more tentative than measures or findings (CIPFA, 1984: 4).

PIs are a logical consequence of the kind of planning model which schools and colleges are being encouraged to adopt. An emphasis on priorities and targets naturally leads to an attempt to formulate related PIs. In the most general sense a PI is an assessment of a specific management or planning objective. Several comprehensive lists of PIs have recently been produced. The DES has published a set of PIs which represents the outcome of collaborative work with a number of LEAs and their headteachers (DES, 1989b). The Training Agency has developed PIs which it is expected that LEAs involved in TVEI will use (TA, 1989a; 1989b). In the further education sector a basic core of PIs is already in use (DES/WO, 1987).

Examination results at 16+ provide the basis for creating perhaps the most familiar PIs in the education service. Results are usually collapsed into a single indicator such as the number of GCSE passes, grades A to C, per Year 11 pupil on roll. Examination success is of course only a partial indication of a school's performance. Good examination performance may indicate more about the quality of the pupil intake than about the effectiveness of the teaching and learning provided. More work has been done on the use and interpretation of PIs derived from examination results than on any other. Attempts to present examination results fairly, so that variations of pupil intake are controlled, continue to exercise the talents of a small number of influential researchers using statistical techniques of analysis and interpretation (Goldstein, 1984; Goldstein and Cuttance, 1988; Gray *et al.*, 1986, 1990).

PIs can be used within both external inspections and self-evaluations as background information and as a means of focusing on specific issues that may warrant more detailed examination. In addition they can be regarded as a separate source of information in their own right. It is increasingly being recognised that effective monitoring and evaluation in LEAs will require contributions from three principal sources of information derived from:

- local inspectors' observations of teaching and learning;
- schools and colleges including the results of internal evaluation;
- sources inside and outside the LEA including PIs.

The Audit Commission (1989a) suggests that local inspectors will play an important part in systematically recording and analysing the information from these three sources to provide informal feedback to teachers and lecturers and formal reports to a variety of audiences, including the LEA and governing bodies.

The integration of these information sources into a unified, coordinated, comprehensive and authority-wide evaluation strategy represents a formidable challenge, which no LEA has yet been able to meet. There are major problems to be faced concerned with the organisational aspects of establishing such an approach as well as methodological ones related to the processes of collecting, analysing and transforming raw data into trustworthy educational judgements. Such problems are not exclusive to the education service. In the training sphere the new TECs will be in a similar position. Although the national inspectorate for youth and adult training schemes – the TSAS – will play an important monitoring and evaluation role, its numbers are limited. It will therefore be unable to cover adequately the full range of schemes. It is therefore likely that the TECs will augment their evaluation capacity through the use of PIs and the further development of the self-evaluation which is already a feature of training schemes. Indeed it could be said that all public services composed of multiple and semi-autonomous units need to develop service-wide programmes which involve internal and external evaluation approaches.

UNDERLYING ASSUMPTIONS

Monitoring and evaluation have increasingly come to be seen as essential parts of the process of managing the education service. Government policy throughout the previous decade has tended to regard the problems of education as amenable to solution by the use of better management techniques. Evaluation and its mirror image of accountability are to be two of the principal mechanisms for ensuring that the education service meets the criteria of the 3 Es – *efficiency, economy* and *effectiveness*. The prevailing educational philosophy is essentially managerialist. More recently, however, that philosophy has been further developed to include an emphasis on the related notions of education as a market and education users as consumers. For those who hold this philosophy, education is no different from any other commodity. Educational institutions are therefore thought to need the bracing and revitalising experience of competing for the custom of educational consumers. This experience, it is believed, will both raise educational standards and ensure the efficient provision of educational services.

The managerialist-consumerist view tends to conceptualise the education or training process in technical-rational terms in which such notions as monitoring, evaluation, accountability and performance are regarded as essentially unproblematic. The underlying philosophy is scientific management which in turn is derived from the more fundamental perspective of positivism. Positivism regards the world as existing 'out there' independently of human beings and governed by discoverable general laws. This perspective is associated with the spectacular rise of the physical sciences in the two centuries or more which have followed the Enlightenment. The model of science became the ideal which the social sciences sought to emulate, as did in turn the study of management, often termed the management sciences. Positivism, however, has been under attack in the physical sciences for many years, particularly in the field of particle physics, where its warrant once seemed most unassailable. It is increasingly recognised that our knowledge of so-called reality is the outcome of the interaction between the observer and the observed and that universal laws do not exist independently waiting to be discovered but arise from the act of participation of observers with and in nature. If this is true of the physical sciences it will be no less true in the social sciences where the objects of study are human beings and their activities.

All of this may seem a little removed from the concerns of those who seek to evaluate educational and training provision.

The point being made is that regarding such notions as performance and standards as unproblematic aspects of objective reality is both naïve and potentially harmful. The performance of a school is not an objective entity which exists outside those individual minds which construct it. Performance is a construction by which we attempt to make some sense of that complexity which we call a school. Holding this view does not necessarily lead to a disabling relativism which renders practical activity impossible. What it does do is to suggest that the constructions of different individuals should be shared, discussed and debated with the aim of producing more sophisticated, more meaningful, more inclusive and more consensual constructions. The aim is not to find some universal truth but to reach greater agreement on how we should make sense of our world in order to provide a firm basis for acting purposefully within it.

The alternative is to seek to impose the constructions of one person or group over those of others. No construction is value-free. Consequently the dominance of one construction is tantamount to imposing one set of values on everyone else. Its imposition then is inevitably a political act. In education the dominant constructions are frequently made by those with power, political or managerial: the government, the DES, local councillors, officers, headteachers.

Evaluation is itself a construction. The dominant version is undeniably a positivist one. This is reflected not only in government policy and DES guidance but is deeply embedded in the thinking of LEA staff and indeed the majority of people in general. So pervasive has been the positivist model of scientific enquiry that it has been assimilated as a taken-for-granted and often unrecognised assumption of commonsense views of the world. The effect has been to regard scientific enquiry as the only valid means of acquiring reliable knowledge. Consequently knowledge which has not been gained in this way tends to be considered suspect and therefore to be rejected. When this view is applied to evaluation the all too likely outcome is an attempt to eliminate judgement as undesirably subjective and unscientific. To do so, however, is to pursue a chimera. No matter to what level of detail criteria are developed, the act of judgement always remains as an obstinate residuum which cannot be explained away. The practice of evaluation then needs to be based on a model of enquiry which is not limited by the narrow assumptions of positivism.

In a democracy the conduct of evaluation should also be consistent with democratic principles. The imperative of management is not sufficient justification for the use of procedures and processes which could result in the undemocratic treatment of employees. Evaluation should be an aid to enhanced accountability within a democratic context and should provide an opportunity to generate information to help in the efficient and equitable maintenance, support and improvement of education. An acceptance of notions like evaluation, performance and standards as unproblematic and definable solely by those with power has the potential for creating instruments of oppression rather than of liberation.

If this is to be avoided the underpinning values of evaluation should be guaranteed by an informed consensus and its conduct must be subject to a set of ethical considerations. Evaluation is ultimately based on the use and transformation of information derived from people. It is essential that individuals have some proper influence over the information which they provide: its nature, how it is collected and the use which might be made of it. Although the question of ethics has been explored by some evaluators (Simons, 1987) it seems not to have been given such explicit consideration by inspectorates.

EVALUATION LITERATURE

Although much has been written in recent years about educational evaluation, its relevance to the concerns of LEAs and TECs is by no means obvious. The examples described in the literature are of evaluations which tend to have the following characteristics:

- *discrete*: not part of a larger evaluation programme;
- *one-off*: not repeatable;
- concerned with *innovative projects,* with a strong bias towards those which are curricular in nature;
- carried out by *full-time* or *near full-time evaluators*;
- conducted over a relatively *protracted period of time*;
- usually set within a *theoretical perspective*.

In contrast, the evaluations of LEAs and TECs are likely to be:

- parts of *whole systems* made up of many individual evaluations;
- *repeatable*: an evaluation of a school may recur in an evaluation cycle;
- more commonly concerned with *existing* institutions and programmes;
- concerned with the *full* range of institutional or programme elements: the organisational, managerial, financial as well as the purely curricular;
- carried out by a wide *variety of personnel*, in most cases as part of their main role;
- conducted under conditions of severe *time-constraint*;
- *atheoretical*: the language of an inspection report usually reflects a conventional educationist perspective.

In other words, the evaluation literature is not particularly well endowed with examples of good practice and theory to help those who have to address the new evaluation agenda. That agenda may be summarised in brief as *system-wide, time-constrained evaluation*. Although this is not a particularly elegant label it does identify the two main characteristics of the approach to evaluation which government policy calls into play. The term 'system-wide' emphasises that evaluation is organised as an integral part of a strategic planning process which is concerned with the development of a whole LEA and its constituent institutions, or a TEC and its component training programmes. Individual evaluations are inevitably time-constrained for two important reasons. The range of potential evaluations is always much greater than the number of potential evaluators. If an evaluation strategy is to be comprehensive in its coverage then the average time given to any one evaluation will be limited. This tendency will be further reinforced by the necessity for much of the evaluation effort to be carried out by personnel who also have other roles or tasks. In the case of those in institutions whose primary function is to teach, the amount of time which can be devoted to systematic self-evaluation will be relatively little.

Those who are involved in time-constrained evaluation cannot easily use the methods of professional or academic evaluators since these require a comparative luxury of time which is not available. For example, to administer and analyse the results of even a single questionnaire or interview schedule may require weeks of a conventional evaluator's time. In other words, methods and techniques cannot simply be taken off the academic evaluator's shelf. At the very least they will need to be significantly modified if they are to be used. In addition, new methods and approaches are needed. Fortunately it is not necessary to start with a blank sheet. We have a long-standing example of time-constrained evaluation represented by the practice of inspection. This is worthy of detailed study not simply to inform the practice of would-be inspectors but to help other educational and training staff who are involved in evaluation activities. We shall see how that may be done in the next chapter.

SUMMARY

Monitoring, evaluation, inspection, accountability are among some of the key concepts involved in the fundamental re-shaping of education and training provision now well under way. These terms are associated with practices and procedures which are often ill understood. Anxieties, misconceptions and stereotypes abound. One of the aims of this chapter has been to attempt a clarification of the terms, to relate them to broader concerns and issues, while at the same time pointing up some of the benefits and dangers of making them operational.

A second major aim has been to suggest that the evaluation task now placed on LEAs and the emerging TECs is of a scale and nature significantly different from that of the past. It poses an enormous challenge to individual and collective ingenuity in translating intentions and aspirations into practice. This is all the more so because the conventional literature does not generally address the new evaluation agenda. The essential components of that agenda are:

- that a new scale of organisation for evaluation is required which is system-wide and which incorporates the regular evaluation of individual institutions and programmes;
- that system-wide evaluation demands the integration of external and internal forms of evaluation with other sources of potentially evaluative information involving the activities

of a diverse range of staff at different levels of the system: officers, advisers, inspectors, managers, teachers, trainers;
- that evaluation at whatever level generates information which is demonstrably useful for accountability and developmental purposes;
- that an appropriate methodology is required which enables trustworthy evaluations to be carried out, inevitably under conditions of time-constraint, by individuals who have multiple responsibilities;
- that a system-wide programme and strategy of evaluation should be consistent with agreed educational values and conducted within an explicit framework of ethical principles.

2

INSPECTION

RECENT EMPHASIS ON INSPECTION

Increased emphasis is being given to the importance of inspection and inspectorates as major means of monitoring and evaluating educational and training provision. This can be seen in the changing fortunes of HMI (Lawton and Gordon, 1987). Since the Second World War there had been a move away from that most familiar of HMI activities, the full inspection. During the 1950s and 1960s the influence of HMI was, perhaps, at its lowest point. Indeed, a Select Committee in 1968 recommended that full inspections should cease and the number of HM inspectors be reduced (HMSO, 1968). However, this was the time when the educational consensus which had lasted from the post-war period began increasingly to fall away. The 1970s were marked by an accelerating disquiet about the state of the public education system, by financial crises and cutbacks in education, and by the emergence of educational accountability as a key issue. In this new climate HMI was able to re-establish successfully an influential national role in which, in particular, inspection was central. Not only was the rate of full inspection increased, but the notion of inspection was significantly extended to encompass national surveys of educational provision and expenditure and the assessment of whole LEAs. The importance of HMI and its inspection activities was unequivocally endorsed by the Rayner Committee (DES/WO, 1982), the most recent of the periodic attempts over the years to review the inspectorate's role. Undoubtedly, the subsequent decision to publish HMI reports on inspections has had the effect of raising the profile of both the Inspectorate and the process of inspection. It is also significant to note that the current complement of inspectors, just under 500, is greater than in the pre-Rayner period.

The notion of a national inspectorate has also commended itself to the MSC. The MSC recommended to the government in 1985 the setting up of a Training Standards Advisory Service (TSAS). The service was established in September 1986 and currently has 44 officers called Training Standards Inspectors (TSIs). The TSAS is responsible for inspecting both YT and ET.

Local government reorganisation in 1974 resulted, *inter alia*, in the establishment of larger LEAs and more coherently organised teams of educational advisers or inspectors. The period which followed has been regularly punctuated by debates reflecting an uncertainty about the exact nature of the adviser role. The government attempted a clarification of this vexed matter in a draft statement on advisory services (DES, 1985). The statement emphasised the function of support and development to teachers, institutions and local initiatives, and the responsibility for monitoring and evaluating the authority's services. Since then, and particularly in the wake of the ERA, the DES has been at pains to underline the importance of the monitoring and evaluation function.

HMI, the TSAS and LEA advisers are but three examples of the several dozen inspectorates found in local and national government. Rhodes (1981) classifies inspectorates as either enforcement or efficiency agencies. *Enforcement inspectorates* are concerned with ensuring compliance with statutory requirements using, if required, action through the courts. Examples include the inspectorates for mines, health and safety, and weights and measures. In contrast, *efficiency inspectorates* are appointed to secure, maintain and improve standards of performance. They do not have legal sanctions available to them and their formal powers seldom extend beyond a basic right to inspect. Consequently, education and training efficiency inspectorates are highly reliant on their powers of persuasion.

THE PURPOSE OF INSPECTORATES

In the Rayner Committee's view, throughout the history of HMI, inspection has been deemed to contain three principal functions:

- checking on the use of public funds;
- provision of information to central government;
- provision of advice to those responsible for running educational establishments.

The first two functions are concerned with issues of accountability and the third with support and development. Although the balance between the functions has varied from time to time, the latter has always been apparent, not least in the substantial in-service programme for teachers which HMI continues to provide. The functions are also regarded as of a piece:

> [Inspectors] would not separate in their minds the function of inspection and advice, consultation and discussion, and would feel that to advise without having first of all inspected, or to set up as consultants without free discussion, would be intolerably arrogant.
>
> (Blackie, 1970: 52)

A similar justification is to be found for TSIs. In the words of their Director:

> We have chosen to call our officers Training Standards Inspectors because only through detailed inspection of a wide variety of schemes can each person hope to develop the basic knowledge that we will rely on to fulfil our role effectively. That said, it is vital that we are not seen as YTS policemen. Our recommendations are advisory, and the executive power in respect of each scheme rests with MSC field staff. Our role is essentially about consultancy both at scheme level, and in our efforts to influence the direction of YTS more centrally.
>
> (Tinsley, 1987: 27)

In the case of LEA advisers, the inspectorial function has been much less clearly defined. The most recent major study of advisers, carried out in 1986–7 (Stillman, 1988; Stillman and Grant, 1989), suggests that there is no single generic adviser. Advisers have not, on the whole, done the same work from LEA to LEA, nor indeed within the same LEA. Beyond the planning of in-service education, there are no tasks common to all advisers. On average, advisers spend less than 10 per cent of their time on formal inspection and the designation of advisers in some

LEAs as 'inspectors' has not necessarily indicated any greater emphasis being given to the task (Stillman, 1989). However, the research on which the Stillman and Grant study was based was carried out before the emergence of the ERA and the situation is changing significantly. Undoubtedly, LEAs face a major upheaval in coming to terms with the monitoring and evaluation responsibilities expected of them as a result of the ERA.

The tension between advising and inspecting is likely to be common to all inspectorates because of their tendency to develop broader and more complex aims, and to acquire additional functions over time (Rhodes, 1981). While this is most evident in the LEA situation, some indication of an emerging conflict between the inspectorial and the advisory roles was apparent in the early days of the TSAS (Murphy and Henderson, 1988). Indeed, as a result of the reorganisation of the TSAS from September 1989 TSIs have a more substantial and clearly defined advisory role.

INSPECTION TYPES

The legal basis for inspection in the education sphere is contained in Section 77 of the 1944 Education Act. Although there has never been a rigid definition of inspection, there are conventions, instructions and guidelines (Browne, 1979). It is possible, therefore, to identify the main general elements which are likely to apply to all inspections whether conducted by a national or a local inspectorate. McCormick and James (1983) include:

- the involvement of experienced professionals who are relatively independent of the institution or programme being inspected;
- the observation of various aspects through formal or informal visits involving one or more inspectors;
- the preparation of a formal report on an institution or programme for those responsible for its management;
- the expectation that inspectors have intimate knowledge and continuing experience of what is inspected;
- the function of not solely pronouncing judgement, but also encouraging and developing the institution or programme.

Brief descriptions of the different types of inspection undertaken by HMI have been provided by former inspectors (Blackie, 1970, 1982; Thomas, 1982) and, more recently, by HMI itself on current practice (DES, 1986a). In the case of the inspection of maintained schools, the following categories are identified:

- *Informal visits* are carried out by inspectors, individually or in groups, and often confined within a single day; no formal report is produced, but they contribute to HMI knowledge of the education system and to publications on provision.
- *Full inspections* cover the whole life and work of the school, including the standards of work in each subject and aspect of the curriculum. A report is subsequently issued.
- *'Short' secondary inspections* deal with the general quality of the school's life, work and organisation, not with individual subjects. The report is briefer than that for a full inspection.
- *Surveys* can be concerned with an aspect of the curriculum, a whole phase, particular year groups or combinations of these. They may involve computer-chosen samples of institutions and lead to one or more reports.

The arrangements for full and short inspections follow a standard pattern, though arrangements for surveys are more varied. A panel of inspectors is involved, led by a reporting inspector who is responsible for the inspection as a whole, including the drafting of the report. The size of the panel will vary according to the type and size of the school and whether the inspection is a full or a short one. A full inspection of a large secondary school will involve twelve or more members. The time spent in the school will range from three to five days, depending on the type of inspection. Before the inspection, information is provided by the school, partly through the completion of standard questionnaires.

While in school the inspectors spend as much time as possible observing the work of pupils in the classroom and elsewhere. In addition, they will talk to pupils and staff, look at samples of pupils' work and attend assemblies, registration and tutorial sessions, and a selection of extra curricular activities. Towards the end of the inspection the findings are fed back to the headteacher and other senior staff. The school is encouraged to identify any factual inaccuracies or interpretations which are considered ill-founded. After the inspection, a meeting with the governing body is convened to hear and comment on the main findings before the report is written. The report appears, if possible, within six months of the inspection. Reports, although they do not follow a standard pattern, tend to contain a number of common elements. In the case of maintained schools, copies of the report are sent to the chief education officer, the clerk to the governors and the headteacher. Fourteen days later the report is published and becomes freely available. LEAs are required to indicate, within four months, what action is to be taken in the light of the report's findings.

The TSAS inspection programme of YT follows quite closely the HMI model of the full inspection (TA, 1988; Murphy and Henderson, 1988). The inspection, however, is usually conducted by a single TSI who collects together details of the scheme and the Approved Training Organisation (ATO) responsible for it. The TSI will have preliminary meetings with TA area office staff and scheme managers to explain the inspection procedure and identify any aspects of the scheme requiring particular attention.* Inspections involve, on average, five days of on-site visits. Large, multi-site ATOs or multi-programme schemes may involve two or more TSIs. During the visit inspectors talk to scheme organisers, trainees, work experience providers, supervisors, off-the-job training providers, tutors and others. At the end of the visit the lead TSI gives an oral report on findings jointly to ATO and area office representatives. An inspection report is then produced, summarising the main findings and setting out the recommendations. Six months after the issue of the report, area offices are approached about progress on implementing the recommendations. Some differences from the HMI model include:

- the rare involvement of more than one inspector;
- more specifically formulated recommendations for follow-up action;
- quicker production of the final report;
- proportionately less time spent on observation of the training/learning situation.

A few LEAs appear to have implemented HMI-style inspections (Winkley, 1985) and others are following suit as a result of the 1988 Act. Apart from full inspections, Pearce (1986a, 1986b) identifies the *review* – usually confined to a department or a section – as another feature of LEA inspections. Dean (1990), however, in her list of seven inspection types, uses the term review to denote an examination of particular aspects of work across a sample of schools. Many advisers would probably maintain that they gain an intimate knowledge of schools more from making a variety of regular visits than from formal inspections. Few LEAs have, in the past, required advisers to record such visits, and even fewer have made any systematic attempt to collate such information to provide an advisory service view of individual schools. Stillman (1989) identifies a bewildering range of methods which chief advisers claim their advisory teams use in evaluating the performance of schools. Thus, information on schools may be directly collected by activities variously described as inspections, evaluations, in-depth visits, surveys conducted through visiting, specific team visits, general team visits, advisory team reviews, chief and senior adviser visits. Stillman also found an even larger number of activities which involve indirect, distant, or school-produced information for evaluation. The package of evaluation methods used differed in number, type and formality from one LEA to another.

INSPECTION AND EVALUATION

Inspection is largely omitted from any consideration in the specialist literature of educational evaluation. Partly as a result, inspection lacks a broadly agreed conceptual and methodological base. It is important, however, that such a base should be developed. There are two principal reasons for this. First, if inspection is to play a substantial role in the future, as seems to be the intention, then it will itself come under greater scrutiny. It will therefore be necessary to set out more explicitly than is the case at present the basis for its legitimacy. Second, although the methods and techniques of inspection have not been authoritatively codified, they potentially represent a body of practical knowledge about how evaluation may be carried out in complex real-life situations. As such, the knowledge is likely to be of use to all – teachers, trainers and others – who wish to implement realistic evaluation strategies in the areas for which they have some responsibility.

It is necessary therefore to find out more about the actual

practice in which inspectors and advisers engage when they are inspecting educational or training provision. The practice, and the often tacit assumptions underlying it, should be examined against the background of the general field of educational evaluation.

The variety of evaluation models and approaches proposed can be located on a continuum with a concern for measurement of quantifiable variables at one end, and an emphasis on rich naturalistic description at the other. Inspection tends to be implicitly regarded by inspectors and others as lying towards the latter end of the continuum.

> HMIs and local authority inspectors and advisers adopt a style which does not aim to evaluate through the use of quantifiable measures but through mainly descriptive and 'connoisseurship' modes of evaluation.
>
> (Kogan, 1986)

The two ends of the evaluation continuum define two contrasting paradigms of profound significance not only for educational research and evaluation but for science and the nature of knowledge generally. These paradigms – the *naturalistic* and *positivist* – can be summarised succinctly in terms of the positions which each adopts on a number of issues (Lincoln and Guba, 1985). Compared to the positivist paradigm the naturalistic paradigm holds that:

- there are multiple constructed realities which can be studied only holistically, rather than a single tangible reality 'out there' capable of analysis into discrete and independent variables and processes;
- in an enquiry the observer and the observed are interactive and inseparable and not independent of each other;
- the aim of an enquiry is to identify working hypotheses which describe the individual case rather than laws and principles which are true anywhere and at any time;
- all entities correspond to a state of mutual simultaneous shaping rather than a series of discrete causes and effects;
- all enquiry is inevitably value-bound rather than value-free.

The practice of inspection can be better understood in terms of the naturalistic paradigm rather than the positivist. Inspections

31

are essentially enquiries in natural settings – schools in operation – which:

- unfold as data are collected and interpreted rather than following a totally pre-determined design;
- tend to use qualitative approaches close to those of everyday life – observing, talking – more often than specialised quantitative methods;
- are able to use tacit knowledge;
- involve a close relationship with respondents;
- express their findings in terms of the particulars of the situation and report in a form with some similarities to a case study approach.

METHODOLOGY AND PRACTICE

In this section I shall interpret inspection, drawing on examples of the practice of HMI and the TSAS, in terms of the naturalistic paradigm. However, an important caveat needs to be made. The argument which follows is not that inspectors are simply naturalistic investigators: clearly both HMI and the TSAS operate under circumstances which are not the same as those of the independent researcher that Lincoln and Guba have primarily in mind. However, what will be maintained is that the naturalistic perspective provides a productive *conceptual* framework for making sense of the inspection process and identifying key *methodological* issues which are typically overlooked.

Natural setting

Inspection is clearly undertaken in the natural setting. The aim is to see the institution or scheme in as normal a state as possible. There are two factors which potentially militate against that. First, the timing of the inspection may coincide with an unusual or atypical situation, for example a whole year group of pupils in a school being involved in examinations. Second, the presence of a team of inspectors must result in a situation abnormal in some ways. The extent of any change will be influenced by how far assumptions about the inspection are shared and accepted by those involved. Noblitt and Eaker (1988) suggest that two basic assumptions underlie any evaluation: that the evaluatees involved will suspend any vested interests and accord the evaluation a special status; and that they accept the evaluation approach adopted. In the case of inspection this means that they are willing to regard inspectors as being independent of the authority structures which affect them professionally, and as potential sources of credible educational knowledge. These would seem to be two essential prerequisites if those involved are to participate in an inspection in good faith and with trust. How far that trust is achieved will in turn influence not only how teachers or trainers behave when inspected but also what they will be prepared to disclose in talking to inspectors.

Time is therefore made available before an inspection takes place to outline its purpose and methods. In the case of HMI this is done through the reporting inspector (RI) making a preliminary visit to the institution. The RI may also indicate a willingness to talk to the staff about the inspection if the headteacher or principal is in agreement. The RI may also make available copies of the DES publications which briefly outline what is to be expected from an inspection. However, even if these arrangements are made, the task of ensuring that all staff, particularly in a large institution, are fully briefed is considerable. In practice, therefore, much will depend on the efforts of individual inspectors to allay fears, engender trust and facilitate a climate of normality during the inspection itself. In TSAS inspections similar arrangements are made by the TSI with the scheme manager and possibly other staff.

However, even with these provisos the naturalistic perspective holds that the presence of an observer will always transform the situation. Observer and observed – even if the anxieties of the kind already mentioned are stilled – will disturb the context. Moreover, observer and observed will subtly interact: if the behaviour of the observed is influenced by the observer then so is the behaviour of the observer shaped by that of the observed. An inspector, then, is inevitably engaged in an interactive process with those involved in an inspection. Consequently inspection is to be regarded as a *joint* enterprise. The outcome should be a *shared* and better understanding by all involved of the complexity of the situation being inspected.

Human instrument

All enquiries require appropriate forms of instrumentation for collecting and recording relevant data. Although other forms of instrument such as questionnaires and tests are not automatically excluded, and may be used where appropriate, a naturalistic enquiry uses the human being as the principal instrument. Such a usage has a long tradition in anthropology and other social sciences where the field study is a dominant concern. Inspections can be regarded as certain types of field study and the activities of inspectors rather like those of educational anthropologists working, albeit briefly, in the unfamiliar culture of an individual institution or scheme. Alternatively, an inspection might be regarded as a kind of investigative journalism. In both traditions, anthropology and journalism, the field notebook is the recording device *par excellence* of the human instrument. Inspectors, like good journalists, act as their own investigating instruments. Operating in this way can have a number of advantages. Inspectors are able to:

- collect information about many factors simultaneously;
- respond holistically to the complexity of events;
- process information swiftly and generate hypotheses and test them out with respondents on the spot;
- follow up the atypical, the unexpected and the idiosyncratic;
- scent a good lead.

Scenting a good lead is to be responsive to *tacit knowledge*. Tacit knowledge is that which is gained intuitively, implicitly and essentially non-verbally. It is contrasted with *propositional knowledge* which is concerned with statements about objects, events and the like which are expressed in verbal and interpersonally shared forms. Tacit knowledge is called into play, for example, whenever we recognise a familiar face in the crowd, immediately appreciate a metaphor, ride a bicycle, behave correctly in an unfamiliar situation, respond empathetically to a new person, experience apprehension and not quite know why. Tacit knowledge is likely to be a recognisable concept to inspectors. The inspector relies heavily on being able to get the feel quickly of an initially unfamiliar situation by responding selectively to a range of verbal and non-verbal cues. 'Having a nose for something' is a commonly used image which gets close to the sense of responding to tacit knowledge. An inspector, however, cannot be content for knowledge to remain tacit. Tacit knowledge must be converted into propositional knowledge so that it can be thought about, tested out, developed and eventually communicated to others.

Although an individual non-human instrument can be developed to fulfil a particular function with a high degree of reliability, there is none that can rival the multifunction potential of the human instrument. The human instrument is capable of infinite adaptation. Of course, in order to achieve that potential it requires a background of appropriate experience and training. With that proviso there is no reason why it should not be progressively refined until it reaches levels of dependability equal to the best non-human instruments – not simply in one area but in several.

Qualitative methods

The main qualitative methods available to the naturalistic investigator are observation, interviews and the analysis of documents and records. They provide the flexibility needed by the human-as-instrument to deal with the complex, interactive multiple realities which characterise the social world. All of these methods are extensively described in the literature of the social sciences. The specific techniques for each of the three methods can be regarded as falling somewhere on a continuum defined by formal and structured approaches at one end and informal, unstructured ones at the other. Inspectors tend to use techniques which are closer to the latter end of the continuum and thus to the ordinary life situation. It is, for example, much closer to the practice of inspectors to say that in the course of inspection they talk and listen to teachers rather than interview them. This sense of being closer to the everyday behaviours of looking and talking is also the result in part of the constraints imposed by time. During an inspection, the inspectors have a lot to do in a few days and move swiftly from one teacher and classroom to another, often with no break. Thus, highly structured observation and interview schedules, even if considered appropriate, would be difficult to use in the intensive and tightly programmed atmosphere of an inspection.

To take an example: an inspector in visiting a classroom would ideally want not only to see the lesson but also to assess pupils' responses by talking to them, perhaps questioning them and looking at their notebooks. It is crucial to talk with the teacher as well to get a view about such matters as the intention of the lesson and the general context of which it is a part. In addition, it may also be necessary to look at the resources available to pupils and the quality of the learning environment in general. All of that might have to be accomplished within a 35 minute lesson before moving immediately to another class and teacher. In such a situation the use of highly structured methods would be impractical.

Some detailed insight into how the ways of HMI might work in practice is provided by Thomas, a former chief inspector. He has suggested that:

> HMIs may make brief notes of what they see and hear, but they are more likely to do this between classrooms, when the act is less distracting. Some HMIs prefer to note things in the order in which they occur, class by class, and sort them out under general headings subsequently. Others start by setting out the general headings and enter points under them as they go. Whichever approach is used, the notes at this stage are usually in a highly abbreviated personal shorthand that allows a fuller account to be written later: the time in schools must be given to looking and listening.

> (Thomas, 1982: 19)

Systematisation of HMI enquiry, then, is initially achieved through the making of field notes. At the start of each day during an inspection HMI can be seen fanning out in all directions from their base camp – the room set aside by the institution for their use – returning briefly to it only for coffee and lunch breaks. Thomas, in the quotation above, suggests two broad strategies dependent on whether organising categories are used while observations are being made or afterwards. Unlike the naturalistic investigator, where the categories are not predetermined but emerge during the course of the enquiry, the observations of an inspector are very likely to be guided from the beginning by some general framework.

Notes of visit

Thomas also suggests that the on-the-spot field notes of inspectors are subsequently expanded into more comprehensive versions. Increasingly these take the form of a *note of visit*. Of late HMI has adopted a standard format for notes of visit so that they can be used across all phases and aspects of education. The basic structure for a note of visit consists of such headings as: institution details; quality of work seen; accommodation; equipment and resources; staffing; staff development; curriculum/course provision; academic organisation; assessment and recording of progress. Guidelines on what might be entered under the headings for visits to institutions within different phases and aspects of education have been prepared. Typically what is written under a particular heading is a piece of descriptive and evaluative text, with the emphasis on the latter, one or more keywords and a rating. Notes of visit are generally made on each lesson seen during an inspection or on any visit made to an institution whether part of a formal inspection or not. Not all of the headings will be appropriate for a single situation and, apart from noting the institutional details and the purpose of the visit, only such headings as are relevant will be used.

The completed notes of visit provide inspectors with a basis for constructing the sections of the inspection report for which they are responsible. In addition, copies of notes are now stored in a central data base to which all HMI throughout the country have access.

Sections of a note of visit are rated on a five-point scale. The scale which is currently used is considered appropriate for any section since it is defined in terms of the retrievability value of the associated text. Thus a rating of 1 corresponds to: *generally good, or with some outstanding features; very useful for retrievers for examples of good practice*. At the other extremity of the scale, 5 indicates: *many shortcomings, generally poor; very useful for retrievers for examples of bad conditions, unsound practice*. The intention is that all five grades should be used (HMI, 1988a).

Condensed fieldwork

The short period in the field which characterises inspections is close to the notion of *condensed fieldwork* as originally outlined by Walker (1980) and used by Stenhouse (1982) as the methodology for his Library Access and Sixth Form Study project (Rudduck, 1984, 1985). The ultra-condensed fieldwork carried out by inspectors, over periods shorter than the twelve days allotted to the institutions in Stenhouse's project, inevitably requires significant modification of any enquiry methods originally envisaged for use over more protracted time scales. Although such modifications have no doubt occurred in practice they appear to have been documented neither in the evaluation literature nor in the in-house handbooks produced by individual inspectorates.

Quantitative data

This section has pointed to some parallels between the activities of inspectors and those of naturalistic investigators, particularly in their use of qualitative methods of data collection. Quantitative data, however, may also be used in inspections. These data may be provided by the staff of an institution or scheme, either before or during the inspection. Typical examples in the case of a school include public examination results, available scores on standardised tests, attendance data of pupils, and much of the staffing and curriculum information provided. In some cases these data will be taken at face value while in others inspectors will do further quantitative work on them. For example, examination data might be recast so that they can be compared with national statistics. Even qualitative data may be converted in part into quantitative form. The descriptive comments made by inspectors may also be quantified.

Purposive sampling

Sampling is a key concept in positivist research where the concern is with a recognisable population of events or entities which it is impossible or impracticable to study in its totality. A sample is therefore drawn by a random procedure so that it is representative of the population. The aim is to be able to generalise the characteristics of the sample to the population. Sampling in this sense does not apply to the naturalistic approach which is concerned less with seeking context- and time-independent generalisations and more with describing the individual case in the full richness of its unique situation.

The identification of institutions and schemes for inspection is not governed solely by considerations of random sampling from the total population. An institution is put forward for inspection by local HMI:

> because it is considered that the institution would benefit from an inspection or may be taken as a useful illustration of an issue or topic considered as currently of importance . . . While it is necessary to draw attention to the unusually good or weak, the ordinary or average is often exemplary and should not be excluded.
>
> (HMI, 1988b: para 7)

Once the process of inspection gets under way then questions of sampling inevitably arise. The period of time in which the inspection takes place constitutes some kind of sample of the total programme of the institution or scheme. An inspection is at best a snapshot of a particular five days in the life of an institution or scheme. There are two fundamental questions which can be asked of an inspection. Is the snapshot recognisable for the period concerned? Given that it is a snapshot and taking account of the particular context of any abnormalities or unusual circumstances, do the people involved recognise substantial aspects of the snapshot as being more generally applicable?

The inspection handbook (HMI, 1988b) gives some general guidance which relates to the issue of sampling. The aim is to try to see at least one lesson taught by each member of staff, although this is unlikely to be possible in a short secondary inspection, which involves only a small team of inspectors, or in a college where the number of staff, full- and part-time, may number several hundred. At the same time it is important to sample the work of pupils or students across the range of ages, abilities and courses. This is accomplished by individual inspectors seeing the teaching associated with their specialist curriculum areas. Inspectors will clearly not be able to see all of that teaching and inevitably will have to operate on the basis of some sampling strategy. The strategy is one which is close to that employed by naturalistic investigators and termed *purposive sampling* by Lincoln and Guba (1985). The concerns of purposive sampling are informational rather than, as in conventional random sampling, statistical. Sampling is not representative but contingent and serial – ideally each element in the sample is selected after the information yielded by earlier elements has been considered. Sampling therefore takes account of the continuous ebb and flow of information and the enquirer's on-going attempts to make sense of it. The approach is essentially one of *maximum variation sampling* (Patton, 1980) where the aim is to obtain the broadest possible range of information. Sampling therefore proceeds until informational redundancy sets in, that is, when the sampling of further elements yields no additional useful information.

Here is how the strategy might be employed in a typical school inspection. On arrival at the institution the inspector immediately goes into a sample of lessons provisionally identified in advance. By the end of the day the inspector will have some impressions of the quality of teaching and learning offered in the curriculum area concerned. There will be some hunches which will need to be checked out, some hints of interesting developments not seen but requiring to be followed up – these and other intimations will suggest which lessons and staff to see the following day. In other words, the sample is continually constructed day by day, and within each day, as the inspector progressively builds up an understanding of the salient issues and seeks to test out emerging hypotheses. The procedure will continue with the inspector extending the sample so that there is a *progressive focusing* on the key issues which, at the end of the inspection, will be fed back to the staff and, much later, will appear in the appropriate sections of the inspection report. Whether or not the process of sampling reaches the stage of informational redundancy before the end of the inspection will depend on the complexity of the issues involved. The inspector, unlike the pure naturalistic investigator, has to work within time limits that are fixed and inviolate.

Inductive data analysis

A central feature of the naturalistic paradigm is that of *grounded theory*. In essence this is theory which follows data rather than preceding them. In conventional enquiry the purpose is to collect data so as to be able to confirm or refute theory. In contrast the predilection of the naturalist is to derive theory from the data by *inductive analysis*. This is because it is held that no *a priori* theory can possibly encompass the multiple realities which will be encountered. The assumption is that the investigator enters the situation with as neutral a stance as possible. The aim is to develop categories, descriptions and eventually theories which are cast in terms meaningful to the respondents. The procedures adopted by naturalistic enquirers have been much influenced by the seminal work of Glaser and Strauss (1967). Their notion of *constant comparative method* has been helpfully elaborated by Lincoln and Guba (1985).

The constant comparative method

The first stage of the procedure involves analysing field notes and appropriate documents into individual units which are recorded on index cards. These cards are coded in multiple ways to include details of the source, date collected and the like. Units can be regarded as basic pieces of information which can stand by themselves and be comprehended by those familiar with the context from which they were derived. The cards are then sorted initially on a tacit 'look alike' or 'feel alike' basis. When sufficient cards have been grouped together on this basis they are examined and an attempt made to describe the properties which characterise the cards. These statements are then combined to form a rule which provisionally defines the *category*. This process is then continued with other categories. When all the cards have been assigned they are examined for their completeness, satisfactoriness and inter-relationship.

The constant comparative method can be extended to cover a team investigation (Lincoln and Guba, 1985). In this it is assumed that all members of the team have initially carried out a categorisation of their own cards. A team leader is appointed who starts the procedure off by selecting and defining the rule associated with it. The leader then asks for a similar category from the rest of the team. Those categories that fit are assigned to the leader's pile. Those that do not are set aside for further examination later. The process continues until all the leader's cards have been assigned. Team members having unexamined categories then assume the leader role in rotation until all the team's categories are exhausted. The whole set of categories is then reviewed along with those cards which have not been assigned to an existing category.

This variant of the method can be discerned in the practice of HMI when dealing with those sections of an inspection report which are constructed from contributions made by some or all of the inspection team. There are two main procedures which operate here. Each section has a lead inspector who, as well as inspecting the area concerned, collects notes from other inspectors who observe features relevant to the section concerned in the course of their inspection activities. The lead inspectors then write drafts drawing on these various contributions. Summaries of the main points are presented at meetings arranged on the Wednesday and Thursday evenings during the inspection week. During these meetings the lead inspectors seek from their colleagues confirmation or refutation of the points made in their presentations and any additional examples and information which should be included. These meetings are chaired by the RI. This role is a crucial one not only in structuring the agenda and guiding the discussion but also in ensuring that consensual judgements are clearly crystallised. The whole process can be regarded as a form of the constant comparative method where categories are shared orally rather than tabled physically as cards.

There is some similarity between the formal and explicit inductive procedures espoused by the naturalist and those employed by inspectors. One significant difference between the two is that the organising categories used by inspectors are predetermined to some extent by the structure required of the final report and, in the case of HMI, by the note of visit format. These tend to reflect an educationist's perspective on an institution or scheme in which organisational management structures and roles are dominant.

Emergent design

In a naturalistic enquiry the design emerges. This follows from the naturalist's view that the multiple realities of the situation, the interactions between the enquirer and the phenomena concerned, and the different value systems involved are so complex and unpredictable that a detailed design cannot be worked out in advance. The design therefore emerges or evolves as the data collected each day are analysed and the implications for the conduct of the enquiry for the next day become clear. The possibility is always there for the investigator to make a major departure from the plan of the previous day in order to follow up a compelling hunch. There is a continual interaction between collecting data, analysing data and modifying the design.

In an inspection the basic design is very largely set in advance. For example, the design of an HMI inspection has to be accommodated within five days, classrooms and other learning sites have to be visited, specific staff seen and so on. However, within such predetermined parameters some design details can be changed from day to day. For example, it might be decided to examine a larger range of pupils' work than had been intended or to extend the normal scrutiny of pupil attendance by including an analysis by gender – all because of tentative hypotheses emerging from data already collected. Individual inspectors have opportunities of sharing their insights informally in snatched conversations during the day and more formally when they meet for the evening sessions. During such occasions a need may be identified for a collective exercise to be carried out the following day in order to pursue a particular issue or to examine a pressing concern.

Negotiated outcomes

The outcomes of an enquiry will typically be expressed in terms of findings, judgements and recommendations. In the case of a naturalistic enquiry the outcomes are subjected to the scrutiny of the respondents who provided the information from which they were derived. The notion of *negotiated outcomes* implies that enquirers are open to the possibility of modifying their views in the light of those of respondents but not that they must be in total agreement about data and their interpretation. Respondents have the right to present views on what the outcomes should be. Enquirers have the obligation to consider these. There are two main reasons for emphasising respondents' rights. First, enquirers are invading the personal space of respondents and effectively taking something from them, for example a representation of some aspects of their behaviour or speech. It would therefore seem morally incumbent on enquirers to check out those representations and the interpretations derived from them with the persons involved. Second, where there is agreement between enquirers and respondents there will be greater confidence in the trustworthiness that can be ascribed to the outcomes.

There are several occasions during an inspection when HMI practice goes some way towards meeting this requirement. After observing individual teaching sessions inspectors will generally discuss with the teacher concerned what they have seen. This provides an opportunity not only to hear the teacher's views on the lesson but also to consider and perhaps reach agreement about the quality of the learning achieved. A more formal opportunity is provided at the end of the inspection when meetings are arranged with the heads of departments or sections which they have inspected. Usually this opportunity is extended, with the head of department's agreement, to all appropriate members of staff. At such meetings discussion takes place about inspectors' perceptions of the work seen. The meeting is potentially a two-way exchange and inspectors may modify their view if the evidence put forward by teachers is persuasive. An important ethical procedure operates during these meetings:

> As a general rule, nothing should be said to the head of department about the work seen that has not already been said to the teacher or lecturer concerned, and similarly nothing should be said to the head or principal that has not already been said to the department concerned.
>
> (HMI, 1988b: para 6)

Towards the end of an inspection there is a comprehensive feedback of findings to the head or principal. In the case of a full inspection of a secondary school, where a large team of inspectors is involved, it is usually necessary to begin this on the

Thursday to allow all the specialist inspectors an opportunity to contribute. The arrangements are coordinated by the RI. Each inspector gives a brief summary of the salient points, concentrating on evaluative rather than descriptive comments. By this stage the inspectorate team will be confident of their judgements and may see the meeting mainly as a feedback exercise. However, it does provide a further opportunity for HMI views to be modified in the light of additional evidence. It is therefore essential that the findings are presented succinctly and that the staff are given adequate opportunities to voice any disagreement they may have concerning individual factual matters and specific judgements made. During the meetings the RI takes notes of the discussion.

At the end of an inspection the RI meets the head or principal to present as a whole the team's findings about the institution, or that part which has been inspected. If specialist inspectors have already reported individually, the RI need be accompanied only by two or three colleagues. The head or principal may invite deputies and other senior staff to the meeting. Frank discussion of HMI's evaluation is encouraged and one inspector keeps a note of the discussion.

> It is essential that the discussion of the points raised should be full and frank, so that any views put forward by the head or principal may, if it seems appropriate, be taken into account when the report is written.
>
> (HMI, 1988b: para 11)

Similar procedures are found in TSAS inspections. At the end of an inspection the TSI will have a further session with the scheme manager to indicate the likely issues which will be raised during the formal feedback session, which normally follows within a few days of the end of the inspection, and which will appear in the printed report.

Case study reporting mode

Naturalistic enquiries are best written up in the form of case studies rather than as scientific or technical reports. Case studies are concerned with single individuals, programmes, events, institutions where the aim is to provide a detailed holistic description. Such studies try to capture the idiosyncratic richness of the individual case and its relationship with its context or environment. The author of a case study recognises the importance of communicating the multiple realities associated with the perceptions of the key actors involved. A case study provides sufficient *thick description* to enable the reader who is familiar with the case to recognise the authenticity of the description. On reading the study, someone unfamiliar with the case should be able to experience it vicariously. Moreover, readers should be able to transfer some of the insights of the study to related cases which are familiar to them. The language in which a case study is written tends to be closer to that of a narrative account than the abstract, anonymous and scientifically objective style favoured by positivist reports.

HMI inspection reports are clearly examples of case studies, where the case is usually an individual institution or programme. In an HMI inspection the aim is certainly to describe the case as comprehensively as possible. For example, in a full inspection the complete range of the institution's programmes, activities and achievements are described, related to its particular context and community, and interpreted in the light of comparable institutions across the country as a whole. Inspection reports may be regarded as portrayals of institutions. They differ, however, from those in the naturalist tradition in at least two important regards. First, the perceptions of the institution which are systematically sought are largely those of the head or principal and the teaching staff and to a lesser extent those of the pupils or students. It is not usual for the views of parents, governors or representatives of the community to be directly sampled. The purpose is not to point up the differences between the perceptions of the institution by key groups but to use such information to validate a perspective which is essentially that of the informed objective educationist. Second, an inspection report eschews the highly personalised accounts that characterise some case studies.

Inspection reports are careful to avoid any reference that can be directly ascribed to an individual teacher. The aim is to describe the teaching, never the teacher. There will be no inclusion in the report of *direct* quotations from teachers and others frequently found in the case studies of educational researchers. Inspection reports therefore tend to lack the compelling readability, akin to that of a good story, that characterises some educational case studies. The implicit model underlying the authorship of an inspection report is that of the detached connoisseur critic.

The raw materials of the report are the draft paragraphs derived from the field notes of inspectors. All inspectors have one day set aside for this task. These drafts are then forwarded to the RI and the appropriate specialist staff inspectors. The latter are able to comment to the RI only on urgent matters relating to these. The RI has up to five programmed days to produce the draft report. There then follows a carefully programmed procedure whereby the draft is submitted to a number of readers both within and without the original inspection team. The report may therefore be revised several times before it is submitted for printing. Much effort is therefore put into the report writing and revision process with very careful attention being paid to language, grammar, conventions and house style.

Similar careful attention to ensuring the correctness of the final report by exposing it in draft form to the scrutiny of others is apparent in the practice of the TSAS. There are, however, some differences between the two inspectorates. TSAS reports identify clear recommendations for follow-up and subsequent action, although these cannot be regarded as mandatory. HMI reports do not have this degree of specificity and the term recommendations is avoided. An HMI report effectively points up for the institution matters which require attention, a series of points for consideration rather than specific recommendations. TSAS reports tend to be shorter and produced in final printed form more quickly than those of HMI, appearing within a few weeks of the end of inspections. HMI reports may take up to six months to appear. This greater time lag is in part the result of the more extended chain of scrutiny which HMI reports receive and the heavy demands made on the printing facilities of the DES. Copies of TSAS reports are circulated to the managing agent, TA staff and the Careers Service. TEC chairmen also receive copies.

Working hypotheses

Naturalistic enquiries express their findings in terms of the particulars of the case rather than in terms of law-like generalisations. Unlike the positivist, the naturalist is sceptical about the possibilities of achieving control and prediction of phenomena through scientific generalisations. The acceptance of the notion of multiple realities and the direct interaction between investigator and context which characterise a naturalistic enquiry logically require that findings are expressed tentatively in terms of *working hypotheses* which are specific to the particular context and time.

HMI practice, particularly as reflected in its outcome as inspection reports, is broadly consistent with the above view. An inspection is a snapshot of the institution concerned. In other words, it provides some kind of picture or portrayal of the institution as it was observed to be during the inspection over a period of up to five days. Of course, however large the team of inspectors it is not possible to observe everything which takes place within an institution, even that part which is the principal concern of the inspection, the formal learning of pupils or students. Inevitably a sample of the learning has to be examined. It is implicitly assumed that the findings from this sample adequately describe the situation of the institution during the period of the inspection. This is essentially a low-level generalisation: the findings from the sample observed generalise to the total population of lessons which took place.

The descriptive and evaluative statements which compose an HMI report tend to have a status lying somewhere between generalisations and working hypotheses. A crucial question is whether the description of the institution provided by the report is applicable only to the period of the inspection or whether it also holds good at other times and indeed in general. For example, does a statement like '*In many classes the teaching approaches rely strongly on exposition by the teachers*' describe a persistent characteristic of the school? The confidence to agree with such a statement will depend on whether there is other broadly corroborative evidence from beyond the period of the inspection. This is often the case. One of the routine activities of HMI in inspections is to review a sample of pupils' work drawn from across the years and the ability range. This

48

enables HMI to see the products of teaching and learning over a much longer period of time than that of the inspection alone. Thus it is possible to discern in pupils' work the effects of undue teacher exposition.

In addition, the teachers will be able to indicate whether descriptions based upon the inspection findings are atypical or not. There is the opportunity for them to do this in the feedback sessions which take place during and especially towards the end of the inspection. There are also other types of observation made during the inspection which can confidently be asserted to describe the situation generally. Physical aspects of an institution, for example accommodation, clearly fall into this category. Thus the reader of an HMI report tacitly assumes that much of the description, while it does not hold for *all* time, nevertheless applies to a substantial period of the immediate past. The report then is not completely time-specific.

In contrast an inspection report is recognised by both HMI and the informed reader to be largely *context-specific*. An inspection report of a school, for instance, is relevant only to that one school and may not necessarily have any significance even for another school of the same type. However, an inspection report may help practitioners in other institutions to relate what they read to their own situations. As Walker (1980: 34) says:

> Generalising ceases to become a problem for the author [of a case study]. It is the reader who has to ask, what is there in this study that I can apply to my own situation?

Generally speaking, HMI present their findings in the context of the institution concerned. We have already noted HMI's reluctance to appear dogmatic or prescriptive. The tentativeness of their judgements may be regarded as an expression of an intuitive naturalistic perspective.

HMI repeatedly carry out inspections up and down the country. Although each one is specific it is a reasonable assumption that different inspections and therefore different institutions will have some things in common. If that is so, then inspection reports can be examined with a view to seeking evidence for the existence of underlying regularities in the hope of formulating, at least tentatively, statements of wider applicability. The results of such a process can be seen in HMI publications which review major sectors of the education service. An example is provided by the study of secondary schools (DES, 1988c). This study brings together the results obtained *inter alia* from 185 short inspections – known as dipsticks – carried out during 1982–6. Almost any of the several dozen findings of the study can be regarded as generalisable for those years to the state of secondary schools as a whole. For example:

> The vast majority of pupils had mastered the skills of reading, writing, discussion and numeracy, but ensuring that pupils could use these skills in contexts other than those in which they had been acquired was generally underdeveloped.
>
> (DES, 1988c: para 58)

Since the sample of schools was selected by random procedures the confidence for effectively generalising the findings to the bulk of secondary schools is strengthened. The sample is, moreover, assumed to be comparable to that used in a similar exercise carried out a decade previously (DES, 1979) since in some cases the findings of the two studies are contrasted. Thus the extent to which HMI statements are context- and time-specific appears to vary according to whether they describe individual institutions or broad sectors of educational provision.

CONCLUDING NOTE

The purpose of this chapter has been to suggest that naturalistic enquiry provides a useful conceptual framework for understanding the process of inspecting an institution or programme. Whatever its form, it should be clear from the analysis which has been carried out that there is not a complete correspondence between naturalistic enquiry and inspection. Nevertheless, the match of inspection with naturalistic enquiry is very much greater than that with conventional positivist investigation. It is certainly not contended that inspection methods must conform exactly with naturalistic ones. What is maintained, however, is that the naturalistic model provides a convenient and effective framework for highlighting key methodological issues about inspection. In doing this it also provides an initial basis for describing the techniques of inspection in greater detail than is usually the case. In addition, it begins to suggest ways in which these techniques might be systematically developed in novitiate inspectors and maintained and further enhanced for experienced inspectors.

In essence the chapter has sought to demonstrate that inspection must be seen in the tradition of qualitative field research. It is from within this tradition that an inspection methodology should be derived. The task, however, is not simply one of incorporating existing techniques and methods of qualitative research into the repertoire of inspectors. Inspectors work under quite different conditions from researchers. In particular they carry out evaluations within time scales dramatically shorter than those of researchers. It will therefore be mainly through a modification of qualitative methods that a developed and credible way of working for inspectors will be fashioned.

Such a way of working will not necessarily exclude the use of quantitative data and methods where these are appropriate. For example, HMI in recent years has sometimes carried out questionnaire surveys of aspects of educational provision to supplement and extend information from individual inspections. Furthermore, quantitative data are usually included in the routine information collected before or during an inspection. The current interest in performance indicators is likely to lead to an enhancement of the quantitative context within which individual inspections will be conducted and interpreted.

*The functions referred to here *et seq.* have now been assumed by the TECs.

3

ALTERNATIVES TO INSPECTION

Inspection is an example of evaluation by outsiders. An alternative approach is evaluation by insiders, by those directly involved in the institutions or programmes being evaluated. Such internal or self-evaluation is often promoted as being more appropriate to occupational groups, like teachers, that aspire to recognition as professionals.

Inspection could also, in principle, be replaced by an external system involving the recruitment of specialist evaluators. This is the situation which operates in the USA where there has never been a tradition of national and local inspectorates. To a considerable extent, HMI and LEA inspectors occupy the role here which external evaluators have across the Atlantic.

The third potential alternative to inspection which has gained credence of late is the use of performance indicators. This represents an attempt to extend quantitative specification from simple inputs to the processes and outcomes of education and training.

The aim of this chapter is to examine each of these three alternatives and to assess the contribution which they can make to a comprehensive evaluation programme.

SELF-EVALUATION

A spate of LEA school self-evaluation schemes was produced from the late 1970s onwards. By 1984 well over half the LEAs in England had instituted their own schemes or were supporting and encouraging individual school initiatives (DES, 1986b). Many of the schemes were similar to each other and were clearly influenced by the format of the ILEA progenitor: *Keeping the School under Review* (ILEA, 1977). They were generally of the checklist type and consisted of a large number of questions covering the main aspects of a school's organisation and activities. Although mainly directed at the headteacher and senior staff, most schemes allowed the possibility of involvement of other teachers. The items required respondents to give short or yes–no answers. Rating scales were also employed in some schemes.

One of the characteristics of most LEA checklists was that they attempted to cover the full range of a school's education provision. James (1981), however, questioned whether evaluation of the whole school was feasible and hence the practicability of those schemes which attempted this. In her view a *gradualist* or *incrementalist* approach was better, where schools evaluated a different part of their work each year.

Although the majority of LEA schemes appeared to have been influenced by a management-by-objectives approach, the details of the assumptions underlying their construction had not been made explicit. As Clift (1981) observed, the schemes tended to reflect the unstated assumptions of LEA officers and advisers about what constitutes quality in education. This lack of rationale arose in part from the fact that, although a great deal has been written on educational evaluation in recent years, much of it is concerned with the evaluation of curriculum innovations. While Shipman (1979), for example, has provided some useful practical guidance on evaluating a school as a whole, there is still surprisingly little in the educational literature concerned with the theory of institutional self-evaluation.

Related to the lack of an explicit rationale in this early phase of the development of self-evaluation was the general neglect of the *process* involved. Process has at least two aspects. First there is the issue of how staff are to be organised so that they can participate in, and contribute to, self-evaluation. Second there is the matter of how the questions raised in a self-evaluation are actually addressed. This opens up the problematic area concerning the collection, analysis and interpretation of appropriate evidence.

LEA schemes of this period can be distinguished according to whether their use was voluntary or mandatory and whether they tended to emphasise a public accountability or institutional development purpose. Two early schemes which illustrate the range which is possible are those of Oxfordshire and Solihull. These have been included in a major study carried out by an Open University team (Clift *et al.*, 1987).The main conclusions of the study were as follows:

- Carrying out a school self-evaluation requires a substantial amount of time, energy and resources.
- School self-evaluation requires that teachers be trained for it. How that should be done is not entirely clear.
- School self-evaluation requires schools characterised by cooperation and open communication where professional development and professional self-respect go hand in hand. Not many schools may match these criteria.
- School self-evaluation is not very cost-effective and certainly never the 'cost-free' means of obtaining school improvement often advocated.
- Provision for school improvement should be included explicitly right from the outset in plans for school self-evaluation.

These conclusions apply to schemes as they were at a relatively early stage in the development of school self-evaluation.

Self-evaluation post-ERA

Most LEAs are now likely to include self-evaluation as a component of their strategy of monitoring and evaluation. LEAs differ, however, in the emphasis which is given to self-evaluation compared to other approaches, that is, to various forms of inspection. Some LEAs have developed self-evaluation instruments. These generally seem to avoid the over-detailed format which was characteristic of schemes in the earlier phase of self-evaluation. There also appears to have been a move away from the comprehensive self-evaluation exercise to one which concentrates on a smaller number of specific concerns and priorities. Some LEAs intend that self-evaluation should be carried out annually on the basis of a regular cycle. This would entail evaluating some aspects of the school or college every year so that over the cycle as a whole – two, three or more years – the full range of activities and programmes would have been involved. In some cases a series of annual partial self-evaluations is intended to be followed by a whole institution review, for example every three or so years. In other words, LEAs seem now to favour the gradualist rather than the total approach to self-evaluation.

One approach which is gaining support is to incorporate self-evaluation within a cycle of development planning. For example, Hargreaves *et al.* (1989) have outlined a practical approach to the production of school development plans. This involves a planning cycle consisting of four processes:

- *audit*: a school reviews its strengths and weaknesses;
- *plan construction*: priorities for development are selected and then turned into specific targets;
- *implementation*: of planned priorities and targets;
- *evaluation*: the success of the implementation is checked.

The purposes of the audit are to clarify the state of the school, to identify strengths on which to build and weaknesses to be rectified and to provide a basis for selecting priorities for development. In order to carry out an audit in a relatively short period of time it is necessary to decide which areas to select and which to postpone for later years. It is recommended that the two areas of curriculum provision and resources should always be included, since they will require annual auditing.

Issues emerging from the audit will be among the factors which will influence the construction of the plan. The plan is constructed in detail for the year ahead; longer-term priorities for the following two or three years are described in outline. The construction of the plan should take account of the views of all staff and should result in the identification of no more than three or four priorities for development. The priorities are then turned into *targets* which specify the *tasks* involved and those who will be responsible for them. A target is both a guide to immediate action and a focus for later evaluation. Targets should identify the criteria by which success in reaching each target can be judged. These *success criteria* are a form of school-generated performance indicators. Targets, tasks and success criteria are incorporated into *action plans* which become the working documents for teachers.

Implementation of the plan is assessed regularly by *progress checks*. These are collated to form the basis of *success checks* to determine how well a target or priority is being implemented. Implementation and evaluation are therefore regarded as integrated rather than separate and consecutive processes. However, a formal act of evaluation – *taking stock* – is carried out at the end of the school year. This in turn prepares the way for the audit which begins the planning cycle for the following year. A full audit covering a more comprehensive range of a school's activities might be carried out every few years. Taking stock provides the headteacher with the basis for making an annual progress report to the governing body.

The processes of audit, taking stock, progress- and success-checking constitute the key features of what is effectively a self-evaluation model. These in turn are incorporated within a more comprehensive model of school planning. A major aim is to maximise the likelihood that evaluation influences action. In addition, self-evaluation contributes to the school's task of rendering an account of its achievements for the year. School development plans may therefore provide a means of integrating the developmental and accountability functions which are seen by some as irreconcilable within a self-evaluation model.

Three major challenges, however, continue to confront those who advocate a central role for self-evaluation. First, self-evaluation has to demonstrate its credibility. Acknowledgement is sometimes made of the importance of providing an external validation of the process of self-evaluation. Moderation, accreditation and auditing are among the terms in vogue. They refer to three different processes. *Moderation*, in this context, implies an assessment by those external to an institution of judgements made by those within it. In doing so an external moderator brings to bear knowledge of comparable institutions and is able to adjust judgements which are considered to be unduly lenient or severe. *Accreditation* is where an institution is approved, for a definite period of time, to carry out its own self-evaluation. The presumption is that the institution has appropriate mechanisms for evaluation and that the outcome of applying them can be accepted with confidence. *Auditing* may be regarded as an external check of the process of evaluation carried out and an attestation of the results obtained. Conducting an external audit in this sense would require the auditor to have access to the original data and other information which had been generated and used in the evaluation. Just as an accountant inspects the financial books of a company, an educational auditor will examine the evaluation documentation and data of a school or college. The procedures for carrying out moderation, accreditation or external auditing in the ways defined above have not yet been worked out in sufficient detail for them to be implemented by LEAs as recognised and acceptable elements of an evaluation strategy.

The second challenge is that self-evaluation is never a cost-free exercise. The involvement of institutional staff means that efforts are redirected, at least for some time, from other tasks, such as teaching, to evaluation. Balancing the opportunity and other costs of taking part in self-evaluation against the benefits to the individuals and programmes concerned is therefore crucial. This in turn requires that the methods used are economic in terms of time and other resources. This is an aspect of the third challenge, essentially methodological, of how to collect, analyse and interpret evidence in effective and efficient ways which command broad acceptance.

EXTERNAL EVALUATION

Mention has already been made in chapter 1 of the growth of external evaluation in LEAs during the previous decade as a consequence of the government's introduction of categorically funded projects. TVEI, the most substantial and influential of these projects, was initially introduced as a pilot scheme involving twelve LEAs. The aim of the initiative, which got under way in 1983, was to explore and test ways of managing the provision of technical and vocational education for those aged 14–18 within the education system. Other LEAs were recruited to the scheme in successive years so that by 1987 almost all authorities were involved. Further development through the Extension Programme (TVEE) was announced in July 1986. This gave to all LEAs from 1987 onwards the opportunity, after three years' pilot experience, to seek funding to extend TVEI across all secondary schools and colleges and to all students aged 14–18. Thus, within five years TVEI effectively became the first nationally sponsored curriculum development project with the capability to involve all members of the relevant age group. With over £1 billion committed, TVEI represents the biggest curriculum development project yet seen in this country.

The national and local evaluation of TVEI

The purpose of this section of the chapter is not to describe the characteristics of the various TVEI projects which national and local evaluation have identified. Rather it is to consider the implications of the latter for the conduct of practical evaluation generally. The concern here is with the methodological lessons which have been learnt. Many of these lessons also emerge from the evaluation of other major categorically funded projects. The justification for concentrating on the evaluation of TVEI lies in the fact that its size, scope and coverage are much greater than those of any other project.

TVEI has become one of the most heavily evaluated curriculum development programmes. The pilot projects in England and Wales were evaluated by two separate research teams – one from the National Foundation for Educational Research (NFER) and the other from the University of Leeds School of Education – each dealing with somewhat different aspects. TVEE is also being evaluated by the NFER. In Scotland, evaluation of TVEI has been undertaken by the Scottish Council for Research in Education. These evaluations have been funded directly by the TA (formerly the MSC). In addition, each individual TVEI project has its own local evaluation funded indirectly through the LEAs using their TVEI budgets.

This pattern of national and local evaluation is common to other categorically funded projects. The funding for evaluation is, however, limited. The national teams have been relatively small and thinly stretched to cover many sites across the country. The organisation of local evaluation has varied from LEA to LEA. The level of resourcing has generally allowed the appointment of only a part-time evaluator, often through the secondment of a local teacher. Evaluation strategies have perhaps been most firmly established where it has been possible to involve academics from institutions of higher education.

Although in the past LEAs had the experience of external evaluators working within their midst, this tended to be of a somewhat different nature from that associated with categorically funded projects. For example, in the era of the Schools Council most LEAs had schools involved in the trials of materials associated with national curriculum projects. Such activities brought project teams and evaluators in contact with teachers and LEA advisers. This experience lacked in general the high political salience and the contractual relationship which characterises the later wave of categorically funded projects. Consequently the reputation of LEAs, their institutions and their staff are felt to be much more on the line than was the case in the earlier phase of curriculum development. The need to be seen to deliver agreed contractual outcomes is paramount. This gives a special prominence to local evaluators and brings them face to face with the power relations in individual institutions and the LEA.

Challenges of the evaluator's role

The new situation represented by involvement in TVEI constituted a learning experience for both evaluator and LEA. Neither party knew what evaluation could do in the new context and the working out of a *modus operandi* has not always been easy. In retrospect it is clear that evaluators should take nothing for granted concerning their sponsors' understanding of evaluation. Evaluators need to negotiate and clarify such issues as:

- what is to be evaluated;
- how evaluation is to be carried out;
- how access to staff and institutions is to be decided;
- for whom evaluation is carried out;
- how the evaluation is to be reported;
- the limits of what can be reported.

In other words the purposes, methodology and ethics of evaluation need to be specified in the form of a clear contract between the evaluator and the sponsor(s). This in turn should be widely disseminated to significant stakeholders in the evaluation.

A dilemma of which evaluators became acutely conscious is whether they were to act in a *formative* or *summative* role with respect to their projects. In other words, were they to provide information to the project to help in its improvement or to make judgements about how good it was? The distinction is of course not clear-cut and evaluators might be expected to do both. The approach of local TVEI evaluators seems to have been largely a formative one. However, as Saunders (1986: 47–8), himself a local TVEI evaluator, points out, avowal of a formative approach may be used as a sign of 'goodness' and a 'central plank in the rhetoric of legitimation'. As he remarks, quoting one TVEI coordinator: 'Evaluators are as likely to say their evaluation isn't formative as a headteacher [is to] say he didn't have the interests of his pupils at heart.'

Combining the two tasks of formative and summative evaluation is not easy, as Fitz-Gibbon (1986), another local evaluator, points out. The implication is that involvement in a formative style may incapacitate an evaluator from acting in a summative way. Pseudo-summative reports may result, lacking a real critical stance. This tendency, she suggests, referring to American experience, may be heightened when project directors hire evaluators known to them or personally recommended to them: 'People rarely pass harsh judgments on friends'. Nixon (1989) stresses the acute awareness local evaluators may have of the heavy accountability demands placed on the projects they are evaluating. Under these conditions, he suggests, there is a danger that evaluation loses its cutting edge and becomes increasingly instrumentalist in its thinking:

> The term 'formative' would thereby come to denote a process more akin to the fine tuning of a machine than to a close examination of the principles by which, and purposes for which, it operates. Evaluation, to draw on the jargon, would have gone 'cosy'.
>
> (Nixon, 1989: 641)

Despite these problems the local evaluation of individual TVEI projects has encouraged a productive relationship between LEAs, schools and evaluators which in the best cases has promoted ideas and principles of cooperative evaluation within and across schools and colleges (McCabe, 1990).

Methodological issues

Projects pose formidable problems for evaluators, not least of which is the fact that they are not single, homogeneous, neatly bound entities. In reality they are multidimensional programmes of loosely coupled activities and developments, operating across multiple sites. The situation is further complicated because the projects may take several years before reaching their full-blown form. Thus it takes four years for a complete cohort of pupils to experience the 14–18 TVEI curriculum. Schools and colleges, moreover, may be recruited to a project over successive years, as in TVEI, so that at any one time institutions will be at different stages of involvement. Projects, although they may be initially fairly tightly defined, inevitably evolve as teachers and others confront the task of translating proposals on paper into actual curriculum reality. Projects do not, of course, operate in an innovation vacuum: there will be other initiatives taking place alongside them. The task of separating the effects is a methodological minefield.

It will be apparent then that the complexity and dynamic quality of projects precludes the feasibility of adopting an experimental design approach to evaluation. Consider, for example, the task associated with identifying a control group of non-project schools. This would inevitably involve trying to match selected institutions on criteria which may not be overt, against a set of comparable schools. In many cases the data necessary to support the likely criteria of comparability – curriculum provision, staff characteristics, innovation climate and the like – would almost certainly not be available in other than the most crude form. The identification of control groups of pupils may be a somewhat easier task. Such groups have been used in TVEI in at least one local evaluation (Saunders, 1986) as well as in the national evaluation (Hinckley *et al.*, 1987). Evaluation designs have inevitably relied on survey methods supplemented by qualitative approaches using interviews and observation, and in some cases incorporating a longitudinal perspective.

Qualitative approaches to evaluation have been increasingly used in recent years. However, despite their popularity we are still far from having an agreed and rigorous methodology to underpin their use. Hutchinson and his colleagues (1988) have emphasised the problematic nature of establishing validity in qualitative evaluations of categorically funded projects. They emphasise, as other qualitative evaluators do, the importance of *triangulation* as a key technique for improving validity. In brief, this consists of contrasting the perceptions of one actor in a particular situation, with those of others in the same situation: the classroom teacher with the pupils, the evaluator as observer. They recommend an extension of this process which would involve the use of other data sources relevant to the situation being triangulated, for example questionnaires, documents.

Tight time scales are a common feature of the evaluation of categorically funded projects, particularly those at local level. This is because funding has been relatively modest and so what might have been better done under more favourable conditions of resourcing has to be telescoped and tailored to meet the limited budget available. This has inevitably meant that evaluators have had to adopt data-gathering methods similar to those advocated by Walker (1980) and which he called *condensed fieldwork*. This approach has been further accentuated as a result of the pressure to feed back results speedily to those working within the project, all of which places a great strain on validity. The response which Hutchinson *et al.* make to this is to generate grounded observational frameworks for condensed fieldwork.

> Upon the basis of our initial observations on, and analysis of, our research we develop a series of categories which seem to us to comprise the reality of the situation we are investigating. These are not *a priori* categories, but the result of . . . observation and analysis . . . . They have therefore emerged from the data. These categories form the basis of our observation schedule. Because we know what we are looking for, having been intimately involved in the evolution and analysis of the categories from the data, time in the field and the number of observations can be reduced.
>
> (Hutchinson *et al.*, 1988: 8)

While observation may be a feature of evaluation designs in this field it has sometimes been a minor one, and greater emphasis has been placed on collecting a teacher perspective by interview. Observation must be central to the evaluation of any innovation which claims to be about the transformation of the educational experience of students. Our knowledge of the reality of classrooms generally is over reliant on information provided by teachers. Hutchinson *et al.* (1988) note from their own experience as local TVEI evaluators that teacher interviews on teaching style did not correlate well with their observational data on this aspect. Responses from pupil questionnaires and interviews, however, correlated far more highly.

Something of the approach recommended above can be seen in the national evaluation study of twelve TVEI schools carried out by the Leeds team (Barnes *et al.*, 1987). This study followed all lessons of each TVEI course in the schools over a two-week period. Lesson observations were taped for later transcription and supplemented by field notes made during the lesson. Interviews were also conducted with teachers and students. Samples of course documents and copies of students' work were collected for later analysis. The methods adopted for analysis and reporting consisted of four stages:

1 Raw data were consolidated into a level 1 archive.
2 Level 1 archive was organised and categorised, with the aid of a wordprocessor, to yield a level 2 dossier. Level 2 categories underwent continual development. They amounted to a set of pigeon holes into which information from level 1 was allocated and from which it was retrieved.
3 A level 3 document was written at a higher level of abstraction than levels 1 and 2. This was fed back to the teachers.
4 Issues were extracted as a basis for reporting. This was undertaken collectively in a series of team meetings. Once issues had been agreed, analysis of data from levels 2 and 3 were undertaken and reports written.

The Leeds research has encouraged studies of classroom behaviour in some local evaluations. For example, Davidson and Parsons (1990) were able to employ a flexible methodology to study the variations in teaching and learning styles in TVEI and non-TVEI lessons. Their approach utilised a combination of a structured observation schedule and field notes guided by an *aide-mémoire* consisting of an organised set of general questions. Research of this kind is important for a number of reasons, not least to demonstrate the lack of shared criteria among teachers and others as to what constitutes good teaching. The vocabulary of teaching styles which characterises TVEI and other curriculum projects often operates at a purely rhetorical level in which commitment to a series of pedagogic slogans – negotiated learning, active learning – masks a lack of agreement about the constructs which underpin them. The researchers argue that:

> taxonomies, typologies and continua will not help evaluations to support development in teaching and learning styles in TVEI until they are expressed in highly specific terms which the teacher can relate unambiguously to his or her classroom experience.
>
> (Davidson and Parsons, 1990: 63)

Large-scale surveys have been a feature of some of the local evaluations of TVEI as well as of the national. For example, surveys of students' views of their pilot TVEI experiences have been carried out (see Hazelwood, 1990; Helsby, 1990). Some of the larger local evaluations, particularly those involving consortia of LEAs and evaluators based in institutions of higher education, have been able to develop strategies combining regular student surveys with interviews of teachers and other key participants (Saunders, 1986).

Evaluations are almost invariably presented as formal reports. In the past these have tended to be relatively lengthy documents, academic in tone and addressed to a general audience. The evaluation reports of TVEI and other projects – both at the national and local level – have generally departed from this traditional format. There has been a conscious attempt to write shorter, snappier, more visually interesting reports directed to the practical concerns of those involved in and responsible for the projects described. In addition, particularly in the local evaluations, reports have been produced at regular intervals rather than solely at the end of the project. The former ensures regular feedback to teachers and other project staff and increases the likelihood that evaluation findings will influence the direction and development of projects. It also allows a strategy of dissemination based on a series of workshops and seminars rather than reliance on a single prestige conference at the end of the project. Feedback and dissemination are not, however, exclusively confined to formal reports and seminars. Local evaluators are able to develop a close and continuous working relationship with projects and may therefore make available their insights to project staff on a more informal and regular basis. However, while there are advantages in this, there is also a danger that evaluators may become too closely identified with projects and thereby jeopardise their critical independence.

Many local TVEI evaluations have been managed and reported as case studies. Case studies are frequently expressed in qualitative as opposed to quantitative terms and generally concentrate on processes rather than outputs. There is a strong tendency for bureaucracies to favour evaluations which produce quantifiable (hard) output data. As Jamieson (1990) implies, the tendency for academic evaluators to present evaluations based on qualitative (soft) data was one of the causes of client dissatisfaction in the early local evaluations of TVEI.

The effect of local evaluations has, of course, been to add to professional knowledge about the development and achievements of individual projects. However, what has been emphasised in this section is the contribution which the efforts of local evaluators have made to a better understanding of practical evaluation – not least to those in LEAs, schools and colleges. That understanding, although undoubtedly variable from LEA to LEA and institution to institution, can be briefly summarised in terms of a more sophisticated recognition of the importance of the political and methodological implications of evaluation. In the case of the former, evaluators and their sponsors have been forced to confront the need to balance the imperatives of two approaches to evaluation. These are the *democratic* approach which insists on the right to know and the *bureaucratic* which justifies itself by the reality of power (McDonald, 1976). This in turn has emphasised the importance of negotiating the conduct, style and findings of evaluation with sponsors and others. The close working relationship of evaluators with projects has also brought a whole range of methodological concerns to the attention of a wider professional audience. In essence these concerns are associated with the attempts to carry out formative and action-oriented evaluation under conditions of condensed fieldwork.

PERFORMANCE INDICATORS

Inspections and evaluations invariably result in the production of reports. Such reports frequently take the form of lengthy, discursive accounts in which descriptive and evaluative comments are interwoven in a complex fashion. Although accounts are often rich in insights, those who have the responsibility of managing the individual institution or programme concerned may find them difficult to use. Their value to those at local or national level responsible, for example, for the organisation of an education service, composed of many institutions and programmes, may be very limited. Up-to-date accounts of the full range of institutions, even if available, would provide such a diverse mass of information that considerable treatment would be required before they were in a form suitable for assisting the planning process.

Characteristics of performance indicators

For management and accountability purposes, attempts have been made to describe the essential aspects of the work of organisations economically in terms of discrete, quantifiable characteristics. An important reason for identifying such characteristics is to be able to make valid comparisons between different institutions and programmes. The term *performance indicator* is frequently used to describe these characteristics. A distinction may be drawn between simple indicators and performance indicators (PIs). Simple indicators correspond to what are usually understood as management statistics. A simple indicator may become a PI when it is related to a specific management objective and a value judgement is involved. Scheerens (1990) defines performance indicators as statistics that allow for value judgements to be made about key aspects of the functioning of educational systems. Included in this definition are:

- the notion of dealing with measurable characteristics of educational systems;
- the aspiration to measure key aspects, not necessarily in depth;
- the requirement that indicators show something of the quality of education.

There is a good measure of agreement about the features which worthwhile PIs should possess. They include (Hulme, 1989):

- relevance to the agreed objectives and management needs of the organisation;
- simplicity and restriction in number consistent with purpose;

- acceptability and credibility;
- usefulness for signposting areas of enquiry;
- where comparisons between organisations are to be made, specificity, quantifiability and standardisation;
- acceptability of cost in relation to likely benefits.

PIs are frequently derived from an *input–process–output* model of organisations. Such a model may be very appropriate to describe the functioning of factories, where inputs are the raw materials which are transformed by successive processes into outputs or products. Each of these three phases can be unambiguously identified and the conversion of raw materials into products confidently controlled. Applied to schools, *inputs* may be identified with the resources of money, staff and non-staff cost items and the raw material of the pupils. Some examples of related indicators might be: pupil–teacher ratio; expenditure per pupil on books; proportion of households with school-age children in which English is not the normal language of communication. *Processes* include the educational activities carried out in the school, both curricular and extra-curricular. Indicators might include: proportion of time devoted to specific subjects; number of hours of homework set per week. *Outputs* are the results and achievements of the school: in the case of secondary schools an example would be the proportion of Year 11 pupils remaining in full-time education in school or college.

The organisation of PIs

In general it has been easier to define input PIs than those representing outputs or processes. In particular, it has proved difficult to specify PIs that relate unambiguously to the aspects of educational provision which people value most: the quality of pupils' learning experience and the nature of the management/leadership of a school. As a result, current formulations tend to consist of lengthy lists of factors which leave the reader with the difficult task of deriving performance indicators from them. The outcome of the DES/LEA project which resulted in a PI *aide-mémoire* (DES, 1989b) illustrates this tendency. Very few of the items listed satisfy the criteria of a good PI described above. Many items consist of purely descriptive statements or general questions, such as: How is the effectiveness of the school's homework policy monitored? Rather than being a list of PIs the *aide mémoire* has an appearance not dissimilar to the kind of self-evaluation document produced by some LEAs in the late 1970s.

The identification of a number of *first-line indicators* (Smith, 1987) is likely to be more helpful for the managers of individual schools or colleges than lengthy PI lists. The first-line indicators would be scanned by managers to identify areas meriting further investigation. If this seemed to be the case then appropriate *second-line indicators* might be examined. This in turn might lead to a more detailed on-the-spot enquiry which went well beyond the consideration of statistical data. A potentially important type of second-line indicator would be that derived from first-line ones by disaggregation. For example, in the case of a secondary school a key first-line indicator might be the number of A–C grade passes at GCSE per Year 11 pupil. Appropriate second-line indicators would be related measures for individual GCSE subjects.

The notion of seeking to identify a relatively small number of first-line indicators has intuitive appeal. When we are asked to describe someone we know well we typically do so with a limited number of descriptors. These are often capable of giving someone who does not know the person an adequate and meaningful portrait. Asked to elaborate further on any one of the descriptors, we draw upon related and more detailed information. A similar economy of description is used when we attempt to portray institutions that we know well. To friends who are thinking of sending their child to the school yours attends, you are likely to find yourself commenting on relatively few but broadly based descriptors: examination results, pupil behaviour, the state of the buildings, relationships with parents and teaching methods. The descriptors that people typically use are often strongly evaluative; they imply the existence of a continuum, and are about things that matter, at least to those involved in the discussion. Performance indicators may therefore be seen as an attempt to make explicit and more systematic the relatively economical descriptions we make of institutions in everyday life.

What I am suggesting is that a detailed set of performance indicators might usefully be organised in a hierarchy of levels under a limited number of first-line indicators. The latter might also constitute a skeletal portrayal of an institution, and in addition would provide an initial basis for planning, management and evaluation purposes, both by those within institutions as well as those outside them. Before developing the implications of this model further it is important to stress, as have other commentators on the field, that indicators, no matter how carefully chosen or finely elaborated, will at best give a crude representation of the underlying reality of institutions. They are but *indications* of what might be. If they do collectively provide a portrayal of an institution or programme then it will be one like a blurred photographic image of something of which the overall shape is nevertheless recognisable. The value of performance indicators is to be judged in terms of how usefully they point to issues and concerns which can be subjected to further examination and follow-up by more sophisticated procedures. The use of performance indicators, then, is possibly a necessary condition for effective management and related activities but certainly not a sufficient one.

Developing PIs

What then might be the first-line indicators of schools? These must be related to the purposes of schools, the fundamental one of which is the transformation of pupils. Schools exist to provide a systematic means of developing in pupils certain knowledge, concepts, skills and attitudes which are deemed desirable. Here lies a major problem. First, there will be differences of view about what these desirable outcomes should be. These differences may, in a pluralist society like ours, be profound. In other words there is the problem of consensus. Second, the range of possible outcomes of education is vast, and many are unexpected and idiosyncratic to the individual. In brief, our ability to predict reliable outcomes of education is very limited, particularly in areas which go beyond the acquisition of factual information.

The way in which educationists have traditionally attempted to tap this vast pool of learning outcomes is through the use of test results and, particularly in the case of secondary schools, the results of public examinations. In fact the latter have generated a set of PIs upon which more work has been done than on any other. Despite that and the concerted efforts of educational researchers, debate continues to rage about how such results should be collected, analysed and interpreted. Tests and examinations assess some of the cognitive outcomes of education but by no means all. Moreover in their traditional form they are inadequate to deal with the subtleties of the affective aspects of education.

The advent of the National Curriculum, however, may improve the ability to measure learning outcomes a little more comprehensively and effectively. This is because pupils will be assessed at ages 7, 11, 14 and 16 on a range of Standardised Assessment Tasks (SATs) for the National Curriculum. It should also be noted that the problem of curriculum consensus referred to above will, as a result of the National Curriculum, have been eased to some degree. The existence of SAT scores for individual pupils should help to reduce one of the major difficulties in using examination results to compare the performance of schools. It has long been recognised, other than by the popular press, that comparisons of results are invalid unless one knows the characteristics of the pupils involved, for these vary widely from school to school. In the past, few schools outside the former ILEA have had reliable measures of the abilities of their pupil intakes. Consequently it is difficult to say, for example, whether the good results of a school are largely due to it having an exceptionally able intake rather than as a consequence of what the school has been able to achieve. At best, schools and LEAs have used measures of socio-economic disadvantage of the catchment area (rather than of individual pupils) – based on census data or the proportion of pupils in receipt of free school meals – as proxies for intake characteristics. In future the SAT scores of individual pupils at 11 will be compared with those achieved at 14 and 16 when they are in secondary schools. We should therefore be better able than at present to assess the specific contribution which the school *qua* school makes to pupil learning, the so-called *added value*.

Other PIs associated with the effects of schooling and amenable to quantification which have been proposed include: destinations of pupils post-16 ; pupil attendance rates; proportion excluded from school; proportion involved in various extra-curricular activities. However, it is increasingly recognised that the relationship between existing performance indicators and the provision of quality education is seldom unambiguous and often obscure.

Some purchase on the elusive entity of quality may be gained by the systematic collection of the perceptions of the clients of education, primarily students and pupils, but also parents and, where appropriate, employers. Some promising developments in the further education sector arising out of interest in the explicit marketing of courses are relevant in this respect. In particular, the Responsive College Project has demonstrated how simple and easily completed questionnaire instruments can be used to gauge the views of students and their employers about the courses which they attend (Theodossin and Thompson, 1987). Analysis of the questionnaires allows the isolation of a number of client-satisfaction indicators related to the course, its content and teaching expressed in terms of ratings on a five-point scale. The aggregation of individual student ratings will generate PIs such as the percentage of students rating course factors as good or very good. Such an instrument could be standardised within an LEA to permit the comparison of students' views on different courses within the same college or between different colleges. Fitz-Gibbon (1989) has derived attitudinal PIs from surveys of A-level students in schools and colleges and also related them to subsequent examination performance. There is no reason why instruments of this kind should not be routinely used in secondary schools and perhaps even with the older pupils of primary schools. The computer technology which is becoming increasingly available to all schools provides the necessary facility for analysis of the data collected.

Similar instruments could be designed to identify teachers' views on the quality of the organisation of the school, the resources and materials provided and the extent to which they facilitate the teachers' ability to provide opportunities for effective learning. The great advantage of sampling staff and pupil views by the use of simple questionnaires is that once designed they can be used on a year-by-year basis. This would enable the derivation of performance indicators on an annual basis. This is particularly important since the implementation of LMS is based on the notion that performance is reviewed each year with the aim of assessing the extent to which resource decisions have affected educational provision and learning outcomes. Questionnaires used for this kind of purpose have other advantages. They provide a relatively quick and not too onerous way of involving, if required, all staff and pupils while at the same time ensuring anonymity. This is particularly important when views are being sought on potentially sensitive issues such as the quality and contribution of senior management or the LEA.

More elaborate questionnaires can be constructed which are explicitly based on models of school effectiveness. The field of *school effectiveness* is represented by a very substantial literature. Oakes (1989) has reviewed much of the American literature and has suggested three global school conditions as ideal targets for PI development:

- *access to knowledge*: the extent to which schools provide pupils with opportunities to learn domains of knowledge and skills;
- *pressure for achievement*: the institutional pressure the school exerts to encourage hard work and achievement;
- *professional teaching conditions*: those conditions that can empower or constrain teachers in creating and implementing programmes of learning.

Oakes goes further and attempts to specify examples of indicators which might be derived from each of the three conditions. For example, under professional teaching conditions she identifies such factors as: teacher salaries; pupil load/class size; teacher time for planning; administrative and clerical support. Questionnaires might be constructed to assess teachers' perceptions of such factors as these in their own schools. Institutional level PIs might then be derived from the aggregation of individual assessments.

Uses of PIs

From what has been said it is clear that PIs alone cannot constitute an adequate system of evaluation. There are two main reasons for this. First, the nature and comprehensiveness of existing PIs are insufficient to deal with the range of issues that are associated with even the simplest educational organisation. Second, PIs do not speak unambiguously for themselves. They need to be interpreted, understood in terms of other information which lies outside or beyond the PIs. They may, however, support or supplement existing inspections or other types of evaluation.

PIs can be used in inspections in two principal ways. They can provide a basis for comparing the performance of an institution with others of the same class. For example, the examination results of a secondary school may be usefully compared to those obtained by schools generally – either within the same locality or nationally. In making such comparisons it is necessary to take account of the particular context of the school. This is not without difficulty as Gray and Hannon (1986) report in their study of the use of examination results by HMI. They suggest that HMI may fail to notice when a school with a poor intake did well. PIs also constitute a potentially valuable supplement to the information about an institution which is normally collected in advance of an inspection. The assimilation of this background material by inspectors helps in providing a preliminary model of the institution and some provisional hypotheses relating to it. This is crucial in ensuring that inspection gets under way promptly and effectively. PIs might form part of a larger statistical profile (see Audit Commission, 1989a: Appendix A) which could be used by inspectors and also by staff in self-evaluation exercises.

As well as PIs being used in inspections they may also be derived from them. In regard to the latter, the practice of HMI is instructive. As was indicated in the previous chapter, HM inspectors regularly make assessments of the various aspects inspected, using both descriptive and rating methods. Separate ratings made of the same aspect in different situations can be aggregated and expressed in terms of the percentages falling in particular categories. Thus in the HMI report on LEA provision for education in 1986 it is recorded that 81.6 per cent of assessments of overall work in schools of all types visited were judged as satisfactory or better (DES, 1987: 9). The same report also gives percentage assessments on other factors, for example provision of non-teaching staff, accommodation and learning resources in schools. These assessments effectively record performance on national process indicators. Local indicators could be developed in a comparable approach by LEA advisers and inspectors.

In addition to their use for evaluation and accountability

processes generally, PIs contribute to two other functions. They are a potential part of the information which is available to assist the functions of planning and development of educational provision. PIs may also be included with other information about education which is in the public domain. They may therefore be used to serve accountability, planning and development, or public informational purposes. Each of these uses may operate at different levels: institution or programme, local or national. The sets of PIs which may be available at any level will need to be carefully interpreted if sensible use is to be made of them.

CONCLUSION

To what extent are the three approaches outlined in this chapter viable alternatives to inspection? Approaches to self-evaluation are likely to become more systematic, targeted and sophisticated than those which were a feature of its first phase of development. However, as already noted, there is a continuing need to resolve the difficult issues of cost, credibility and methodology inherent in self-evaluation. Moreover it still has to be demonstrated that self-evaluation, even if developed to meet accountability and development needs of individual institutions, can also satisfy comparable needs at the LEA level. Self-evaluation is probably better regarded as complementary to inspection than as an alternative to it.

External evaluation has undoubtedly been an acceptable alternative in the context of assessing the progress and achievements of categorically funded projects. These have generally been specific innovatory projects which have been developed over a span of one or more years. They have also reflected major national educational policies. For these reasons, and also because of their scope and range, they have justified separately established evaluations. Such longer commitments to the evaluation of specific innovations may be less easily tackled by a local inspectorate and are better carried out by evaluators specially appointed for the purpose. External evaluators have made a significant contribution to the level of evaluation knowledge and expertise available within LEAs. In addition, they have pointed the way towards the development of methods capable of meeting the shorter- as well as the longer-term information needs of institutions and their LEAs. However, the use of external evaluation to cover, from year to year, the full range of an LEA's general monitoring and evaluation concerns is likely to prove more expensive than that of a local inspectorate or advisory service.

Performance indicators, certainly at present, are not a feasible alternative to inspection or indeed to self-evaluation. For them to become so would require a significant development of their nature, scope and range as well as more knowledge than we have at present of how they are actually used in practice. In this context it is noteworthy that the DES is interested in the possibility of generating *expert systems* based on PIs. However, even if such computer-based systems are successfully developed it is unlikely that they would render on-the-spot evaluation, whether carried out by external or internal personnel, redundant. PIs are better seen as adjuncts to inspection and self-evaluation rather than substitutes for it.

In conclusion, self-evaluation, external evaluation and performance indicators are three important components, along with inspection, of a possible LEA evaluation strategy. How these components can be brought together at the institutional and LEA levels is the subject of the two chapters which follow.

4

TOWARDS A SYNTHESIS

As noted in chapter 2, the research carried out on advisory services in the period preceding the passing of the ERA would seem to indicate that the field of LEA evaluation was in considerable disarray. One of the effects of the Act has been to force LEAs to face the contradictions and conflicts inherent in the process of bringing their traditional practice into line with the new evaluation imperative. The indications are that the majority of LEAs still have a long way to go in resolving and reconciling the tensions associated with the latter conjunction. At the present time the primacy given to inspection by the DES vies for position in an evaluation spectrum with a less clearly emphasised role for self-evaluation and an uncertain contribution from performance indicators.

There is an urgent need to locate the purposes, methods and organisation of evaluation more soundly within the context of the concerns of the post-ERA LEAs and their institutions. This in itself, however, is insufficient to ensure an adequate rapprochement between the existing disparate elements of a potential evaluation strategy. We have already seen in chapter 1 that the dominant view of evaluation is essentially positivist and provides an inadequate basis for understanding educational processes in general or evaluation in particular. It is therefore necessary to base the notion of evaluation on an alternative set of assumptions which better square with the complexities of actual educational institutions and programmes.

Although this chapter is specifically concerned with the evaluation challenge faced by LEAs, the provisional synthesis which is proposed is of relevance to national inspectorates and also to the likely needs of the new TECs. For the latter:

A systematic and comprehensive approach to evaluation is needed because it will provide a much fuller picture of progress towards objectives, and the relevance of these objectives, than can be obtained from performance indicators alone. Each TEC will therefore need its own evaluation strategy which it will review and update annually.

(TA, 1989c: 12)

THE FUNCTION OF INFORMATION

LEAs must become adept at managing in a pluralist environment where powers and responsibilities are shared – upwards with the Secretary of State . . . downwards with individual schools, colleges and their governors, and outwards with parents and other interested parties from the community.

(Audit Commission, 1989b: 1)

LEAs are thus squeezed from three directions. In adjusting to this pressure they will need to undergo a significant shift of emphasis and change of orientation. In brief this will mean showing a concern for: strategy not detail, management not administration and service not power (Thompson and Parison, 1989). The first two of these lead to the adoption of a *strategic management* stance. The third signifies a move from the traditional LEA role of control to one concerned with the *management of influence* (Ranson, 1988). The former may be said to constitute the primary responsibility of the new LEAs and the latter the style in which it is to be exercised.

Strategic management is derived from the idea that an organisation should be seen as existing within, and affected by, an external environment. The environment consists of relevant institutions and groups and the effects deriving from macro-level phenomena such as economics, demography, technology and markets. Strategic management is the attempt to handle the environment to ensure the survival and growth of the organisation. In the post-ERA situation strategic management should be the central task of those in schools and colleges no less than those in the education departments of LEAs.

Strategic management requires availability of reliable information in order to carry out systematically the following responsibilities at LEA, institutional and programme level:

- policy formulation and planning;
- advising, supporting and improving educational provision.

In addition to an implicit strategic management role, the ERA is also concerned to increase public accountability and to encourage choice. Information is therefore also necessary for:

- accounting to the LEA and its electorate, the governors of schools and colleges, and the local community for the quality of education provided;
- helping people to make considered choices among the range of educational opportunities on offer.

The generation of information should be subservient to these four functions.

INFORMATION AND KNOWLEDGE

The inspection activities of HMI constitute an important means of collecting information on the education service. This information is recorded and eventually transformed into reports on various institutions, services, programmes and projects. These reports implicitly claim to provide educational knowledge. A distinction may be made between information and knowledge. Information may be regarded as the relatively separate and discrete details or items which are collected during an inspection, notes made by inspectors on individual lessons, summaries of pupil attendance. In contrast, knowledge represents the organisation of these details into a structured, coherent and larger whole. This is not simply the result of a crude aggregation of the elements. Processes of analysis, synthesis and transformation are involved so that the end product is a more inclusive and comprehensive conception. For example, an inspection report aspires to describe and explain an institution or programme as a totality and should give the reader a sense of knowing the institution concerned.

HMI reports then are sources of knowledge about the education system. Reports concerned with specific schools or colleges also contribute to a potential knowledge base of an individual LEA. Since the number of institutions in an LEA inspected by HMI in any one year is small the contribution which their inspections make to local knowledge is inevitably limited. An LEA will therefore need to rely on sources other than HMI to generate the bulk of information about its educational provision. Much of this should be provided through the monitoring and evaluation activities of an LEA's own advisers or inspectors. In addition to formal inspections advisers typically visit institutions for a variety of purposes. In the past, however, most LEAs have not required advisers to write descriptive or evaluative accounts on all or most of these visits (Audit Commission, 1989a).

A similar situation applies to the visits made by a wide variety of LEA officers and other personnel. Much of the potential information gained in this way is stored in people's heads and is therefore unlikely to be shared and subjected to scrutiny by others. The golden rule should be that every visit results in some kind of record being made. This is justified on several grounds. Making a record is both an expression of professional etiquette and a recognition of the importance of the visit. Recording also helps the processes of clarifying what actually transpired during a visit and communicating the consequences to those concerned. The record need not be lengthy, indeed often may be quite brief.

Individual institutions will also generate information about their own activities and programmes. This will include a whole host of detail on staffing, curriculum, pupil/student and financial matters which will inevitably become both more detailed and more organised as computerised information systems are installed. This information will be drawn on for constructing a wide range of internal school documents. They will have an authoritative status as knowledge of the institution. In addition to this on-going generation of information, more formally structured special exercises may be carried out, a review of the whole, or a substantial part, of the educational provision of a school or college. Although this may draw on existing information it is also likely that further material will be collected through structured methods involving questionnaires and interviews. The reports produced by such self-evaluation exercises may be seen as another source of trustworthy knowledge.

The nature of some of the information collected by institutions will be determined by national or local concerns. LEAs will require from their schools and colleges a variety of information, particularly of a management and financial nature. Included here will be details of key institutional characteristics with performance indicators expected to play a prominent role.

Educational research traditionally claims a special place as a source of educational knowledge. Much of the activity of researchers is inevitably conducted within LEAs. Typically LEAs and their institutions have had little influence over the design, aims and methods of research carried out by external investigators in their midst. Furthermore, they may have received little or no information feedback during the conduct of the research. Of course, the release of information may sometimes not be feasible because of methodological or for ethical reasons. The possibilities of negotiating such release with the researchers and others involved are worth exploring for most projects. Although LEAs will tend to have much more influence over research which they directly fund very few, apart from the former ILEA, have been able to develop substantial research programmes.

Perhaps it is evaluators rather than researchers who have made the more significant contribution as sources of information on local educational provision. Leaving aside the question of whether or not evaluation is a form of educational research or an activity distinct from it, it is undoubtedly the case that TVEI, LAPP and ESG evaluators have provided a wealth of information about individual institutions, particularly in the context of their ability to implement change.

The sources of information potentially available within an LEA can be summarised briefly as follows:

- monitoring/evaluation and other visits made to institutions and programmes by advisers, inspectors and officers;
- statistical and other returns made by institutions;
- information initiated by the institution: internal reports, governors' reports, self-evaluation reports;
- research and evaluation of specific LEA projects or local versions of national initiatives (TVEI, ESG projects);
- external research involving institutions in the LEA;
- HMI reports on individual institutions and programmes in the LEA.

The degree of influence which an LEA has on such matters as the nature of the information collected, the methods of collection, and access to information and its use, broadly decreases going down the list. The major on-going sources will be the first three.

In the past the information used by LEAs for policy and planning purposes was largely statistical in form. This source will in future be augmented by the incorporation of LEA and institutional PIs. These are likely to be key elements within the general information systems which have emerged in recent years as a result of developments in information technology and the move towards a more managerial orientation for education. Another significant addition will be a pupil database which enables an LEA to aggregate SAT scores and examination results at LEA, sub-LEA and institutional levels.

Typically, however, these six sources of information have been regarded as separate unconnected entities. They need to be seen – and used – as an integrated *information system*. Before turning to the organisational issues involved in establishing an information system it is necessary to consider the issue of *trustworthiness*.

CRITERIA FOR TRUSTWORTHINESS

As we have seen, the function of information and of the more general bodies of knowledge which are derived from it is to serve four important purposes. These may be succinctly summarised as policy formulation, support and development, accountability and providing an information service to the citizenry. On the decisions taken on each of these aspects hang the fate of individuals and institutions. It is essential, therefore, that decisions are taken in the full light of available information. A necessary condition is that information and knowledge must be trustworthy. Trustworthiness, for the purposes necessary here, can be defined in operational terms. Information is trustworthy if it is recognised that it is usable by practitioners on the one hand, in helping to manage, deliver, be accountable for and improve educational services, and by the public on the other, in helping to understand and choose between various educational opportunities.

The usability of information and knowledge is determined by the extent to which they are perceived to satisfy certain criteria. First there is the question of the *impartiality* of those who collect the information. That of HMI is to a very large extent based on its independence. Although the work of HMI reflects the priorities of the Secretary of State, HMI decides what to inspect and how to inspect it. HMI reports as it finds. While the decision whether or not to publish the results of inspection lies with the Secretary of State, anything that is published must be as HMI wrote it. Another factor which helps to guarantee the independence of HMI, and thus the impartiality of its judgements, is that it is not involved directly in the management of the institutions and programmes it inspects. HMI therefore has no personal or professional stake in them and is not beholden to those who are responsible for their management.

This situation does not hold for LEA inspectors and advisers who often manage programmes and projects and, though not responsible for the management of schools and colleges, may be very closely involved through their specialist or general support activities. This may lead, as is sometimes suggested, to advisers inspecting aspects of provision in which they themselves have been heavily implicated through giving advice and support. Questions of conflict of interest may therefore arise and could weaken the claim to impartiality. Anxieties of this kind presumably lie behind the following comment of a former Permanent Secretary:

> Can we be confident that inspection will not be constrained by blueprints of good practice or particular axes to grind? We expect local inspectors to report what in their professional judgement they find – just as HMI do.
>
> (Hancock, 1988: 2)

An LEA therefore needs to be able to demonstrate that the evaluations which are made on its behalf are as far as possible impartial, and not subject to the pressures of local political, administrative and institutional self-interest. A useful general principle might be that impartiality is more likely to be observed the less closely the evaluator is professionally involved with the institution or programme being evaluated. This would suggest that external evaluation of an institution is generally less open to the charge of partiality than one which is carried out by its own staff. In the end, however, the accolade of impartiality is only likely to be accorded after repeated demonstrations of its presence in individual cases.

Systems of collecting information and generating knowledge must have mechanisms for regular review and updating to ensure that they are *current*. Knowledge that has become out of date and fossilised may all too often be used by LEAs at the present time. One manifestation of this is the institutional stereotype arising from perceptions of irrelevant past practices and personnel. The creation of information is not a one-off job. The characteristics and performance of institutions may change significantly even within the space of a year. It is therefore necessary to envisage much of the information available to an LEA being renewed on at least an annual basis.

Ideally information should be *comprehensive* – at the macro-level covering all institutions, services, programmes and projects of an LEA. This is a formidable challenge and is unlikely to be met by sole reliance on a classical inspection approach. At the micro-level, information should be available on all major aspects of each individual institution. This might be realised by the regular production of a basic core of PIs supplemented from time to time by information from other sources.

Information needs to be readily *accessible*. In the case of practitioners this requires information to be efficiently organised in an appropriate format. Traditional filing systems, no matter how well maintained, are not amenable to access by many people on a regular basis. The widespread penetration of computer technology into education now makes multi-access information systems a practical reality. The use of computers determines to a considerable extent the format in which information is recorded and stored. While some types of information will be of a quantitative nature, and therefore appropriate for computer storage, other types will be less compatible. Included in the latter will be the heavily verbal reports which are typical outcomes of inspection. While storage of these is possible they will take up excessive amounts of computer memory. The use of skeletal summaries of inspection reports based on rating key characteristics is a way of overcoming the problem.

Access to information by the public will be largely dependent on the efforts of LEAs and their institutions. They will need to provide information in easily understood forms made available by post, through advertisements and articles in the local press, and the use of local radio and TV. A populace which is becoming increasingly familiar with accessing public computer systems for a wide variety of information may soon demand a comparable facility for educational information. We may perhaps soon see the appearance of the educational equivalent of automatic cash points outside LEA offices, schools and colleges.

The production of information must be *cost-effective*. A system in which vast resources are expended to yield information which no one uses is clearly an extreme to be avoided. That said, it is difficult at the present time to give precise guidance on how performance against this criterion might be assessed. This is because information has not generally been conceptualised in the manner suggested here. As a result, costing the provision of information and assessing its impact have not been attempted by LEAs in the past. Some staff will be heavily involved in information collection and transformation, some might spend much of their time inputting information and generally maintaining the system, and some, for example, classroom teachers, might be periodically involved in information-related tasks at the institutional level as relatively minor aspects of their main role. The new financial sophistication engendered by the ERA will almost certainly make the costing of such contributions possible and may provide a spur to attempting the much more difficult task of assessing the effects of information production and provision. For the time being then it will be sufficient to note that quality information systems cannot be established and maintained without proper funding.

Carrying through the sequence of processes leading to the generation of trustworthy knowledge requires the application of *appropriate methods*, both acceptable to and understandable by practitioners and public. It is here that we face a potentially difficult situation. The methods used to generate knowledge through inspection and self-evaluation are not widely understood and may be dismissed as being subjective rather than objective or scientific. The latter viewpoint reflects the pervasive positivism which constitutes the dominant everyday philosophy of contemporary society.

Evaluation and related terms such as performance, standards and accountability are constructions which are formed to make sense of the situations in which educators find themselves. Such constructions are inevitably shaped by the values of the constructors. If the constructions and values are those of the evaluator alone, then the values of others involved in the situation are effectively denied and evaluation is revealed as an arbitrary political act. Evaluation should therefore be conceived of as an *interactive* process which involves the evaluator and others having a stake in the evaluation. The aim should be to develop *consensual* constructions of greater meaningfulness and inclusiveness so as to provide an agreed springboard for action in the improvement of educational practice. This conception runs counter to the positivist ideal of the evaluator standing outside the situation, neither influencing it nor being influenced by it, and claiming to report objectively the way things really are.

Evaluation is grounded in, and is an extension of, the everyday judgements which we all make when we think about people or things. If someone or something is known to us we can usually render an appropriate evaluation: 'X is a good school, because it gets good exam results and many pupils go on to higher education'. We can conceive of an evaluation spectrum with everyday judgements at one end and the more formal and research-style approaches at the other. Research-style evaluation refers to the relatively lengthy investigations carried out using specialised techniques and methods, and operating within a particular conceptual framework.

Unlike professional or academic evaluators, inspectors are required to operate under conditions of extreme time-constraint: even the full inspection of a school is carried out and completed within a period of five days. Although the evaluation of categorically funded projects has resulted in a significant contraction of traditional evaluation time-scales, sometimes of several years' duration, they are still relatively protracted in comparison with inspections. Inspection is an example of what may be termed *time-constrained evaluation* (TCE). It can be thought of as being located within the evaluation spectrum defined by the poles of everyday judgement and research-style or protracted evaluation.

The conditions under which advisers and inspectors operate as evaluators are likely to be similar in a number of respects to those of other practitioners who are required from time to time to carry out evaluations as part of their normal duties and within tight constraints of time and resources. These will include teachers, senior staff of schools and colleges and education officers. TCE may be regarded as an attempt to systematise and refine everyday judgement by making explicit the processes involved and the assumptions on which it is based. Time-constrained evaluators will draw on the methods of research-style evaluation but will inevitably shape them to the exigencies of the conditions within which they work.

This section has been concerned with the nature of educational information and knowledge and their claim to trustworthiness. It has been indicated that trustworthiness is influenced by the extent to which information and knowledge are impartial, current, comprehensive, accessible, cost-effective and produced by appropriate methods.

The last of these is considered to be especially important. The methods used in what is being referred to here as time-constrained evaluation have not been authoritatively documented. Moreover they are likely to be regarded with some scepticism by those with a more conventional view of evaluation. It is argued, however, that a repertoire of such methods will be needed if the new system-wide evaluation programmes of LEAs are to become a reality. This is because the major components of these programmes, the evaluation of institutions, will be carried out by staff inevitably using TCE, whether through inspection or self-evaluation, even if not recognising it as such. Developing the TCE repertoire is the task addressed in chapters 6 to 9.

ORGANISATION OF INFORMATION

Figure 4.1 shows how information sources and uses are mediated by an information system. Information is collected and is ultimately transformed within the information system into reports, written and oral, formal and informal, for different recipients and audiences. The transformation of information in this way relies on processes of recording, analysis, synthesis and interpretation. Typically not all of the outcomes of these processes will be stored in a central information system. For example, in an inspection the raw field notes will generally be retained by the individual inspectors concerned, though some derivative of these may be stored centrally.

Although an inspection report may be stored after its issue

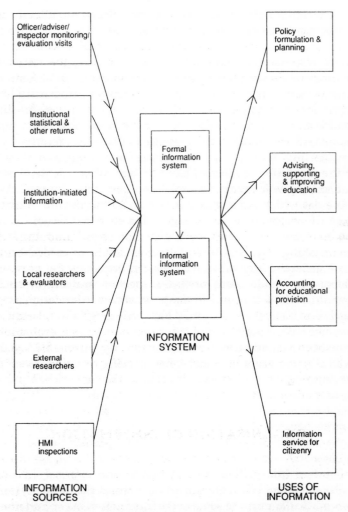

Figure 4.1 **An LEA information system; sources and uses**

to the institution or programme concerned it will generally be preferable to retain a summary only. This reduces the potential load on computer memory and also provides information in an amount and format likely to be more useful for planning and other purposes at the LEA level. HMI practice again provides an example. After an inspection is completed, HMI produces for its own use a summary version based on the completion of a questionnaire which allows individual aspects of the inspection to be rated on a five-point scale.

There is not necessarily a 1:1 correspondence between a particular information source and an outcome. A report may draw on information from several sources. For example, an LEA might wish to have a report on the quality of pupils' experience in a particular curriculum area. This could be drawn up utilising available information from recent inspections of schools supplemented by details from aggregated curriculum returns.

Much information will be stored within the human computer: in the memories of officers, advisers and others. Some of this information will become consolidated over time, by cognitive processes which are largely obscure, to add to the individual's store of professional knowledge. This store is drawn on all the time and may often be much more significant in decision making than the information available in external and more generally accessible systems. On occasions the personal sources are made more public. Inspectors and officers may sometimes find it useful to share whatever information on a particular institution each may have. Although the institution may not have been formally inspected it will in all probability have been visited on different occasions by various LEA staff. Even if these visits have not been formally recorded, some of the information will remain in individual memories. Making these personal information sources accessible to colleagues enables their validity to be checked out and may also lead to a more developed collective understanding of the institution. Some practical ways of carrying out this process are outlined in chapter 7.

The two information systems, *formal* and *informal*, interact with each other. When an individual accesses the formal system for a particular purpose some of the information may be retained within the informal system. The converse is also true. In the past LEAs may have relied excessively on the informal system, the contents of which remained largely covert. The demands of strategic management and a climate of informational *glasnost*, which a more consumerist philosophy encourages, will necessitate a shift in the balance towards greater use of the formal system. The informal information system will, of course, continue to exist. Indeed the more effective the use made of the formal system the more enriched will be the informal system.

It is, however, the formal information system which is the more capable of being organised. The formal system can be envisaged as consisting of a central LEA information base and a network of information bases maintained by each institution, service and major programme.

A guiding principle would be that the central base would store only core information, that necessary for LEA-wide planning, development and policy formulation. Detailed information would be maintained by individual institutions. It would be necessary for the LEA to access institutional bases on occasion to supplement its information in order to carry out central functions of resource allocation, provision of in-service training and the like. At the present time this would probably take the form of the LEA issuing some kind of information return. The development and extension of computer systems, however, will increasingly make electronic accessing the norm.

The core information on individual institutions might take the form of a profile composed of agreed educational statistics and performance indicators. The core could also be augmented by aggregating the judgements of advisers and officers on a variety of aspects of provision made during their visits to institutions. Practice of HMI has shown how this can be done to produce assessments of standards and trends nationwide. The procedures could equally well be used by local inspectors and officers to generate LEA-wide assessments.

The argument so far has been to suggest that monitoring and evaluation are a major means of generating the information which is needed at LEA and institutional level for the purposes of strategic management. The next chapter describes how an LEA-wide evaluation programme, encompassing all institutions, can be established so that appropriate information is generated for the various purposes for which it is required. Before moving on to that issue it is necessary to relate evaluation to the growing interest in the concept and practice of quality assurance and its potential relevance to education.

QUALITY ASSURANCE IN EDUCATION

Of late several LEAs – for example, Berkshire, Kent, Strathclyde – have reorganised their education department structures under a *quality assurance* (QA) rubric. Quality assurance is a key concept in a whole quality lexicon which is the subject of an international standard, identical to the British Standard BS 5750 (BSI, 1987a). BS 5750 was written with the needs of manufacturing industry very much in mind. Its purpose is to inform suppliers and producers about the elements of the management systems which are necessary to deliver quality products or services. There is a growing interest in applying BS 5750 to the public services (see Ellis, 1988) including education and training.

Quality in this context is defined in BS 4778 as the 'totality of features and characteristics of a product or service that bears on its ability to satisfy stated or implied needs' (BSI, 1987b). Most organisations produce a product or service which is intended to satisfy the needs or requirements of users or customers. Quality may therefore be equated with the satisfaction of customer needs. A *quality system* is 'the organisational structure, responsibilities, procedures, processes and resources for implementing quality management' (BSI, 1987a).

QA refers to 'all those planned and systematic actions necessary to provide adequate confidence that a product or service will satisfy given requirements for quality'. The requirements of particular relevance to our concerns here are: *inspection* and internal quality *audits* and *reviews*. Inspection includes 'activities such as measuring, examining, testing and gauging one or more characteristics of a product or service and comparing these with specified requirements to determine conformity' (BSI, 1987b). Inspection will be carried out on incoming materials and services, the process itself and the finished product. Inspection together with other BS 5750 requirements – control of non-conforming product, quality records, statistical techniques and corrective action – constitute the familiar functions of *quality control* (QC). This provides the means for the improvement of process operation.

All elements, aspects and components of a quality system should be internally audited and reviewed on a regular basis. The aim of an audit is to determine whether the quality management system is being operated according to the written procedures. Personnel carrying out an audit should be independent of the specific activities or areas being audited. The findings of audits should be submitted in report form for the consideration of the relevant staff. Reviews will draw on the findings of audits and should be well-structured and comprehensive evaluations. They tackle the wider issues of the overall effectiveness of a quality management system in achieving stated quality objectives.

It is important to recognise that BS 5750 does not set the standards appropriate for a particular quality system. This is the task of the customer or client. It also does not describe how the various requirements are carried out in practice. These will be determined by the customer and/or the supplier. What BS 5750 does do is to set out the necessary requirements which must be met in some appropriate way if a good-quality management system is to be established.

QA: applications to education

Despite its initially unpromising language, with its bias to manufacturing and service industries, BS 5750 does have some potential value for the fields of education and training. It places the responsibility for quality on those who actually control the work. They are influential in defining their own quality policy and objectives. They carry out self-evaluation through internal inspections, audits and reviews.

Inspection can be regarded in the educational context as equivalent to such activities as teachers' routine assessment of pupils' work (testing, marking) and the consequent adjustments made to the teaching and learning approach.

An internal audit is concerned with the extent to which methods used adhere to documented procedures. For example, is the content of a syllabus being adequately covered? A review is a more substantial exercise, carried out periodically to assess the effectiveness of the whole system. Even where internal audit and reviews are in place, external verification will be necessary. This can be considered to occur when an LEA inspection of a school or college takes place.

The relationship between customer and supplier in the commercial world has a parallel in the world of education and training. Schools and colleges may be regarded as *suppliers* of educational services. The *customers* are pupils and students and those who act on their behalf or have a special interest in their progress. In supplying educational services, individual institutions must observe the requirements of national legislation and relevant LEA policies. Subject to these limitations, a quality assurance approach in education would seek to match the service offered to the needs of the customers. This would necessitate:

- collecting information to identify the needs;
- formulating criteria appropriate to the needs;
- determining the extent to which the needs are satisfied in practice;
- seeking improvements where the service fails to meet the specified criteria.

These tasks would be accomplished by internal inspection, audits and reviews.

The staff who work within an organisation act both as internal suppliers and as customers. Such customer/supplier chains can be broken at any point by one supplier not meeting the requirements of the customer. Figure 4.2 represents the school as a supplier/customer chain.

In a secondary school the headteacher and senior staff are suppliers of resources and management services to the heads of departments. The latter, in turn, supply materials, facilities and guidance to their teachers. Teachers are the suppliers of teaching services to the pupils. A recognition of the customer/supplier chain extends the notion of evaluation from the classroom to a consideration of the effectiveness of middle and senior management.

SUMMARY

Monitoring and evaluation are frequently interpreted in a narrow and unsympathetic manner. The purpose of this chapter has been to offer a broader understanding in terms of several potentially unifying themes which are summarised below. Although these themes have been illustrated in an educational context they are equally relevant to the training field. They will therefore be of particular interest to those in the new TECs with responsibilities for developing an evaluation strategy.

- Monitoring and evaluation constitute major means of generating information and knowledge which claim to be trustworthy.

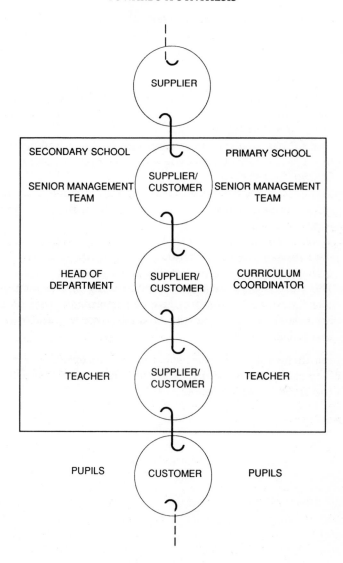

Figure 4.2 **The school as a supplier/customer chain**

- Information and knowledge are essential to the task of strategic management.
- Monitoring and evaluation and other sources of information should be regarded as an integrated information system and organised as such.
- An information system may be conceptualised in terms of two interacting entities: a formal information system and an informal information system.
- The formal information system can be organised in terms of a central information base and a network of institutional information bases.
- The criteria for trustworthiness crucially include the nature of the methods used for collecting, recording and transforming information.
- These methods, which can be generically classified under the rubric of time-constrained evaluation, are consistent with a view of knowledge as consensual construction.
- The various manifestations of monitoring and evaluation – inspection, self-evaluation, use of performance indicators – are related to the concepts of quality control and quality assurance.

These themes provide the basis for the conceptual and methodological synthesis which is set out in more practical detail in the chapters which follow.

5

SYSTEM-WIDE EVALUATION

The discussion of evaluation carried out so far, culminating in
the provisional synthesis set out in the previous chapter, can
be reduced to two basic concerns: the macro-organisational
and the micro-methodological. This chapter focuses on the
first of these – how to organise a system-wide evaluation
programme. The second concern, how to carry out individual
evaluations under conditions of time-constraint, is addressed
in chapters 6 to 9.

LEAs are complex organisations made up of hundreds of institutions as well as dozens of services, programmes and projects.
The range of potential *evaluands* – that is, entities which can
be evaluated – will always exceed the level of resources and
personnel available. Decisions must therefore be taken about
evaluation priorities. Although total evaluation coverage is not
possible within any one year, something approximating to such
an ideal can be achieved by conceiving of an evaluation programme as extending over successive years. The particular
evaluands of one year are in part determined by those sampled
in previous years. *Priorities, sampling* and the notion of a *rolling
programme* are therefore among the key organising principles of
an evaluation programme.

Evaluation priorities can be of two types. There are those
priorities which may be termed *variable*, which change from
time to time as new policy initiatives emerge. Then there are
those which remain priorities for a prolonged period and may
therefore be called *continuing*. The monitoring and evaluation
of institutions is an important continuing priority and an LEA
needs to determine how it will tackle this priority before it
can consider what other priorities should be included in an

evaluation programme. The assessment of institutional performance is the essential core of an LEA-wide evaluation programme.

EVALUATION OF INSTITUTIONS

Self-evaluation, audits and reviews

A quality management perspective (BSI, 1987a, 1987b; Oakland, 1989) on institutional evaluation would emphasise the importance of regular review and audit. A distinction can be made between audit and review. An *audit* sets out to establish whether a system is being operated according to documented procedures. A *review* addresses the much wider issue of whether the system is meeting requirements and is effective. Those who have a quality management perspective are likely to be at one on the issue of institutional performance with those who advocate a self-evaluation approach. It is also difficult to see how the process of regular review, necessitated in particular by the annual budgetary cycle of LMS, would be possible unless the institutions themselves play a major role in the monitoring and evaluation process. Certainly the task of regularly monitoring and evaluating the performance of the several hundred institutions in the typical LEA could not be accomplished by the exclusive use of an HMI-style full inspection approach. Although reviews and audits are seen as internal operations, the quality assurance model assumes that they are carried out independently by staff not having direct responsibility in the areas being audited. This requirement gives greater credence to the claim that reviews and audits are conducted impartially.

The issue of impartiality

There are several options open to an LEA seeking to resolve the dilemma of impartiality. One is effectively to ignore it, and maintain a separate inspection scheme. This is to accept tacitly that self-evaluation serves a developmental rather than an accountability function. A second option relates self-evaluation to a cycle of inspections. For example, self-evaluation may be carried out annually but with an LEA inspection of each institution taking place once every few years. This provides an opportunity for the view of an institution, built up by its staff through experience of self-evaluation, to be compared with that of inspectors. An inspection offers an opportunity for staff to reassess their evaluative skills and thus be more confidently equipped to carry out future self-evaluations. A third option is that inspectors audit the self-evaluations carried out by institutions. The aim of such an external audit would be to attest to the adequacy or otherwise of the methods used in the self-evaluation, the trustworthiness of the conclusions drawn and the judgements made. The auditor would probably also have a moderating function, of suggesting that adjustments be made to judgements where these were thought to be inappropriate or incorrect. The auditor would need to have full access to all evaluation documentation as well as to raw and reworked data.

Given the relatively small number of potential auditors and the large number of institutions, it is highly improbable that external audits could be carried out on every self-evaluation. One possibility would be to have an audit cycle, with some institutions being audited each year – the aim being to cover all institutions over a number of years.

A variant of this approach is *accreditation*. Accreditation might be bestowed after one or more successful external audits. It would be an expression of confidence in the ability of an institution to carry out impartial self-evaluation by trustworthy methods. Accreditation would be for a prescribed period, at the end of which the self-evaluation procedures would once again be audited and a further period of accreditation granted. The assumption is, of course, that there is a generally agreed methodology for carrying out educational auditing and accreditation. This is not the case. Auditing and accreditation, like other vogue concepts in education, tend to be ill-defined and based on limited actual practice. Further consideration of this topic is given in chapter 9.

The use of externally derived information within self-evaluation provides another possible method which, although falling short of a developed model of auditing, goes some way towards meeting the criterion of impartiality. Information of this kind can arise from several sources. For example, a research study within a school may have been carried out which could illuminate a particular evaluation issue. More common perhaps will be the exercises, such as surveys, carried out by the LEA. Their results may enable a school or college to compare itself with similar institutions. Reports by advisers and others as a result of visits made to institutions provide another potentially rich source of external information.

Using the results of self-evaluation

Monitoring and evaluating institutional performance are useful at two levels of organisation – the individual school or college and the LEA. To be useful at the LEA level, self-evaluation should be capable of generating information which can both contribute to a profile on each institution and be aggregated across institutions. This information, moreover, needs to be expressed in a concise form so that the strategic management function of the LEA is illuminated by an understanding of broad trends, themes, patterns and factors, rather than being overwhelmed by a mass of disparate detail. The traditional way in which the results of self-evaluation have been communicated, as discursive reports, while no doubt useful to the institutions concerned, has been of limited value for LEA strategic planning.

The potential usefulness of institutional self-evaluation for LEA purposes can be increased in at least two ways. First, the incorporation of self-evaluation within development planning will help, since the attainment of individual priorities can be more precisely defined and communicated, often in quantitative form. Priorities, however, will vary in nature from institution to institution and will collectively be very numerous. They would therefore need to be reported under a limited number of agreed broader categories. The degree to which the priorities were attained might be assessed on a simple rating scale. For example, a secondary school may have as one of its priorities for the year the introduction of an improved health education programme in the lower school. This priority will be translated into specific targets and action plans which will be communicated in detail to the governors. However, as far as the LEA is concerned it may be sufficient to attest and report the priority under some such category as 'cross-curricular theme' and to indicate whether it was fully, partially or minimally achieved.

A second way would be to encourage institutions, wherever

possible, to report the outcome of their self-evaluations by using appropriate performance indicators drawn from a standard list. Such a list would be compiled in conjunction with institutions and would contain agreed indicators which had been tried and tested. The list would be regularly reviewed and updated as new indicators were created and found to be useful and as old ones became less satisfactory or relevant. In addition, an LEA might wish to specify a number of indicators which all institutions of a particular type would use. These would consist ideally of a mix of input, process and output indicators chosen to give an at-a-glance profile composed of items common to each institution. The indicators would also be capable of aggregation across institutions. The latter facility is particularly important in order that trends and variations can be discerned and individual institutions compared to ones similar to themselves. Pupil–teacher ratio is a familiar example of an indicator which can be aggregated in this way. This common core of indicators, the composition of which might vary from year to year, would be augmented by others related to the priorities specific to individual institutions.

Inspection visits

Self-evaluation, even if modified in the ways suggested above, is insufficient on its own to meet the LEA's responsibilities for monitoring and evaluating the performance of institutions: the potential range of curricular, organisational, financial and other information necessary for an LEA to fulfil its strategic management role is too great. A programme of regular external monitoring and evaluation is also required.

There are two broad ways in which this task can be carried out. One is to organise a regular cycle of institutional inspections carried out by teams of inspectors. The so-called full inspection may attempt to deal with the full range of an institution's activities and programmes; smaller inspection teams will concentrate on a less extensive range of concerns. Full and partial inspections allow an in-depth examination of an institution to be made and benefit from the collective experience which a team of inspectors brings to the task. They are highly labour intensive and have to be planned well in advance. Their excessive use may therefore restrict the flexibility of an inspectorate team to respond to other evaluation priorities which may emerge from time to time.

The second general approach is through a planned programme of individual inspectorial visits to institutions where the focus is on specific specialisms. For example, a geography inspector might systematically visit, for one day or several, all the secondary school departments teaching the subject. To underpin this a programme of visits might also be arranged to examine how geographical topics were taught within the curriculum of a sample of primary schools. Individual visits based on curriculum specialisms would not cover the complete range of institutional concerns. Some inspectors having a more general remit might visit to examine aspects of organisation and management.

Information obtained from individual visits can be used in several ways. It may be fed back in the form of a short report or record to the institution, where it may influence the development of the particular aspect inspected. It may also contribute to the stock of externally determined information which may be drawn on during a self-evaluation exercise. At the LEA level it may provide the basis for some later follow up in the institution concerned. Finally it may be aggregated with information from similar institutions, and thus contribute to understanding how a particular aspect of provision varies from institution to institution.

A further advantage of a programme of specialist visits is that it could be extended to include the visits made by a variety of other officers. With the advent of delegated budgets, officials other than inspectors may well need to visit schools as LEAs develop the requisite comprehensive and sophisticated system of financial monitoring and support. Given the expectation that managing budgets locally will lead to opportunities to improve the quality of teaching and learning, it is essential that visits made by advisers/inspectors and financial staff are coordinated, and that information is shared.

Organising inspection programmes

The monitoring and evaluation of institutions has traditionally been carried out by inspection, most clearly seen in the practice of HMI. The starting point of the HMI programme is a determination of priorities. This is influenced by three factors: government policy and its development; issues and trends arising from discussions with ministers and DES officials; and issues arising from the field. The Senior Chief Inspector (SCI) and the Chief Inspectors (CIs) take account of all these and, after appropriate consultation, formulate a set of overarching *issues*. These issues are few in number and fairly general in form – for example, standards in schools. They are identified in the light of the manpower available and not all issues will be pursued. It is the CIs who decide which shall be included and which discarded.

The issues are then analysed into a larger number of more specific *objectives*. An example might be the quality of pupils' response as indicated by attendance, behaviour and discipline. This activity is carried out by CIs in consultation with Staff Inspectors (SIs) and results in an agreed set of objectives. The full list of objectives is then made available throughout the Inspectorate and bids for specific *tasks* to meet these objectives are sought, such as: identify LEA and school responses to the problems of behaviour and discipline. Each objective has a liaison person assigned to it to act as a contact point for any HM inspector interested in it. The bids are submitted on a standard form which sets out the objective(s) to be met, methods and manpower to be used and expected outcomes. The bids are then scrutinised by CIs to ensure that geographical, phase and subject balance is appropriate and that manpower is deployed cost-effectively.

The bids are then individually and collectively costed and adjusted to ensure best value for money. This costing is done in advance of the DES estimates in order to ensure accurate forecasting of financial arrangements. Inspection is relatively expensive, although not necessarily more so than the alternatives. A self-evaluation exercise of comparable comprehensiveness to an HMI full inspection would not be cost-free, since the opportunity costs of involving a large proportion of a school staff in this way might be very substantial. Furthermore, any attempt to estimate the value of inspections should take account of the likely costs of not having access to the information which inspections provide. Nevertheless, the cost of inspections is not inconsiderable. It is therefore crucial that they are well planned, with clear expectations concerning their outcomes and benefits.

The task of fitting all the bids together and determining the details of timing and the deployment of manpower is a complex task which is carried out by a small *work programme team* composed of four HM inspectors and support staff based at the DES. Details of the work programme, in the form of a computer printout, is issued to every inspector each term. This identifies every inspection event, the dates on which it will be carried out and the names of the inspectors taking part. The arrival of the programme confirms for inspectors the details of their work in the term ahead and effectively constructs much of the detail of their diary. An important element in the work programme is the *milestone* system. Milestones represent a recognition that an inspection involves inspectors spending time on important tasks outside the period actually spent inspecting. The work programme therefore identifies particular days, the milestones, on which specific inspectors will be engaged on the various stages involved in the production of a written report. The implementation of milestones has not only made it possible to give truer costings of the inspection process but has enabled the publication time-scale for the production of a report after an inspection to be cut by half.

HMI experience has considerable significance for LEAs. The first lesson to be learned is that an inspection programme must relate unequivocally to corporately determined *priorities*. In other words, an inspection programme must have a clear justification in terms of issues and concerns that are widely recognised as important. The second lesson is that an inspection programme has to be *planned*. This in turn means determining in advance when particular inspection events will take place, how long they will last and which inspectors will be involved. There has to be an expectation by all concerned that, once the inspection programme is determined, it goes ahead. This requires that inspectors accept the discipline of having diaries structured to a considerable degree by corporate rather than personal priorities. It also means that officers and committee members have to learn that advisers and inspectors should not be pulled off existing commitments in order to tackle other tasks. Advisers have often been the victims of a crisis management model of LEA administration. The model for LEAs should be one of strategic management. This implies planning and *predictable* delivery. A third lesson is that individual inspections must be *programmed*. This entails determining not only when an inspection shall take place and for how long but also the time for carrying out such post-inspection tasks as report writing and editing. Finally, the comparison with the HMI experience helps to clarify the purpose of an inspection programme, and the identity of its *primary* clients. The purpose for HMI is to describe the condition of the education service nationally; the primary client is the Secretary of State. The purpose of an LEA inspection programme is to report on the condition of the education service within a particular locality; the primary client is the LEA and the CEO.

Resourcing an inspection programme

Figure 5.1 shows how the level of resources available for institutional inspection can be derived from the total amount of inspector resource.

Resources, in inspector days, are first split between evaluation tasks and non-evaluation tasks. The latter refers, in particular, to such activities as the provision of curriculum advice and support. These in turn, excluded from the figure to avoid over-complication, lead to further resource decisions and systematic programmes of curriculum development and in-service provision.

Resources are not completely allocated to planned evaluations. A proportion is left unallocated so as to be able to deal with unforeseen evaluations. An evaluation crisis may emerge unexpectedly and the system requires some flexibility to be able to deal with it. A major proportion of the resources for planned evaluations is allocated to the monitoring and evaluation of institutional performance. The remainder will be allocated to other evaluation priorities, discussed in the section which follows. Finally, the resources for institutional monitoring and evaluation are divided between four approaches: full inspections, partial inspections, planned individual visits and support of institutional self-evaluation. The balance between these will vary from one LEA to another according to their

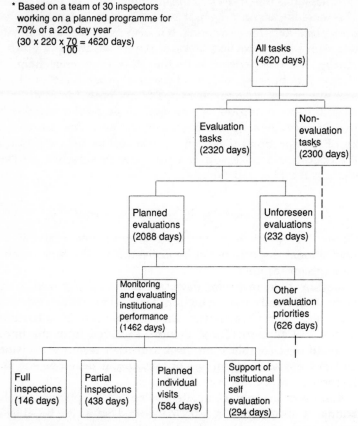

One example of how 4620 inspector days
* could be allocated to different tasks.

* Based on a team of 30 inspectors
  working on a planned programme for
  70% of a 220 day year
  $(30 \times 220 \times \frac{70}{100} = 4620 \text{ days})$

Figure 5.1 Allocation tree of inspector resources

basic evaluation philosophies and the level of resources available to them.

OTHER EVALUATION PRIORITIES

The discussion so far has concentrated on the monitoring and evaluation of institutional performance. It has been suggested that this is one priority among others in a possible LEA-wide

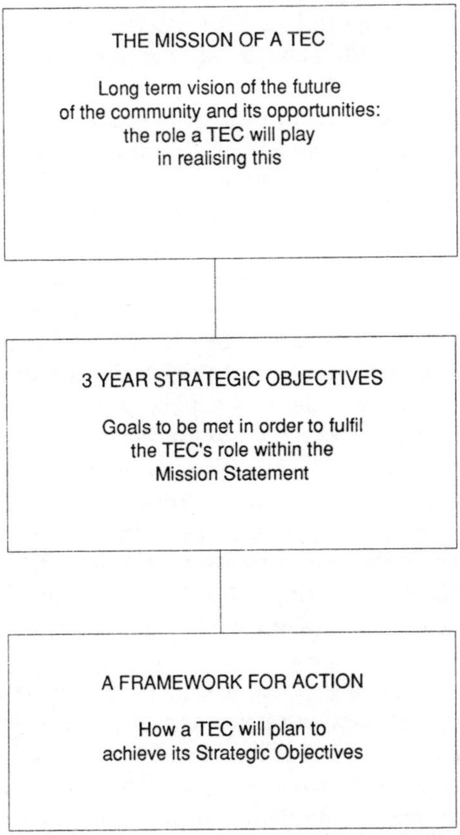

THE MISSION OF A TEC

Long term vision of the future
of the community and its opportunities:
the role a TEC will play
in realising this

3 YEAR STRATEGIC OBJECTIVES

Goals to be met in order to fulfil
the TEC's role within the
Mission Statement

A FRAMEWORK FOR ACTION

How a TEC will plan to
achieve its Strategic Objectives

Figure 5.2 The rational planning model
Source: TA, 1989c

evaluation programme. It is, however, a sufficiently important
and continuing priority to require a substantial and developed
programme in its own right. A comprehensive evaluation programme will nevertheless consist of other continuing priorities
as well as some variable priorities.

Evaluation priorities should ideally be derived from more
general LEA priorities which in turn reflect a mix of national
and local policies. The link between the two sets of priorities
is essential to help to ensure that the evaluation programme
is owned by the LEA as a whole and that its outcomes are
available both to influence the further development of policy
and to contribute to the mechanism of public accountability.

A major intention behind the ERA and other related government policy is to install the same kind of rational management and planning model in education and training as is presumed to operate in commercial and industrial organisations.

A recent example of the model – in this case applied to TECs – is illustrated in Figure 5.2. The *mission statement* is an expression of a vision of the future, the priorities related to it, the role played by the TEC in bringing that future about and the means to be used in doing so. The *strategic objectives* are the medium-term steps to be taken by the TEC in fulfilling its role within the mission statement. They are to be measurable in terms of either numbers or the achievements of a defined milestone, achievable within a given time-scale, and explicitly linked to the mission statement. A *framework for action* focuses on how the strategic objectives are to be achieved, showing what milestones will be reached and by when. The framework for action will include, *inter alia*, an evaluation strategy. Planning models with similar characteristics to the above are now beginning to become more common in LEAs following the ERA. As yet few LEAs appear to have developed a linked *evaluation* strategy, although an increasing number have an *inspection* programme under way.

Evaluation priorities should ideally be defined in conjunction with the more general priorities and objectives deriving from the mission statement. To illustrate how evaluation priorities might be generated, consider an LEA which is poised to reorganise its post-16 educational provision by implementing a tertiary system at the beginning of the following academic year. A useful way to begin would be to review the strategic objectives proposed for the new tertiary system, and to ask the question: What information is needed year by year in order to be able to assess the achievement of these objectives? This would lead to posing the more specifically focused question: What information, if any, is needed over and above that which would normally be available within the system? This might identify issues and informational needs that suggest a broad evaluation priority. This in turn might be reviewed in the light of a more stringent question: What information, if available, would have the greatest potential for remedying any major weaknesses in the system or, better still, indicating ways in which the system could be significantly improved?

The outcome of the proposed scrutiny might lead to the identification of an evaluation priority concerned with the quality of
the student experience in different categories of course. Other
potential evaluation priorities could be obtained in this way by
reviewing the full range of the LEA's strategic objectives. The
end result could be a list of evaluation priorities somewhat too
numerous to tackle which could be further prioritised using a
three-point scale of importance. Each selected priority would
then be considered to identify the nature and scope of any
evaluation and the level of resources, human and material,
which could be made available. The purpose would not be
to spell out the complete range of potential evaluation activity
within the LEA but to identify a relatively small number of
priorities which might be translated into major evaluations.

The initial compilation of a list of evaluation priorities might
be the task of a small group of officers, inspectors and advisers.
The group would carry out much of the preliminary analysis
and would recommend a set of evaluation priorities to the appropriate LEA committee responsible for the strategic plan. The
final outcome would receive the endorsement of the education
committee.

Other contributions to an evaluation programme

As mentioned in the previous chapter, evaluation may also be
carried out:

- by officers and other staff – for example, school psy-
  chologists;
- by collecting information from relevant institutions;
- by the appointment of evaluators to specific initiatives;
- incidentally as a by-product of the activities of HMI and
  external researchers.

Deriving an evaluation programme in the way proposed has the
advantage of increasing the likelihood that individual evaluations are related closely to issues of a practical and policy
nature. However, experience suggests that the maintenance of
that relationship is always problematic. It is therefore desirable
for each priority to have an associated link person who has a
real interest in it and a commitment to utilise the evaluation

findings. Several such link roles could be combined in one person, who might also have responsibility for the coordination and oversight of the whole evaluation programme. A substantial number of LEAs have of late appointed a specialist inspector, usually at senior level, with some such designation as 'monitoring and evaluation'. Such an inspector might very appropriately assume the kind of coordination and promotion role proposed.

The development of an information system

An evaluation programme is a major means of generating trustworthy information and knowledge about the educational institutions and programmes of an LEA. The central base of an information system would be located within the education department and would contain data and information on each of the LEA's institutions and major programmes. In essence, the information base would consist of a series of files or archives, one for each institution and programme. A central information base of this kind, or rather a series of separate bases, exists in an embryonic form in LEAs at the present time in their teaching and other staff; on the physical condition of building stock; possibly, on the school curriculum.

These and other examples of existing information and data bases tend to be:

- a mix of manual and computer systems;
- organised in different ways;
- located within separate sections of the education department and thus accessible only to those within the sections concerned.

The exercise of strategic management at the LEA level requires a unified information base which brings together sufficient details and data to form meaningful profiles on each institution and programme. Such profiles should be useful to a variety of education department staff. The components of the profiles would be expressed, where appropriate, in quantitative terms as performance indicators and management statistics. Some components, however, might need to be stored as brief textual descriptions. The strategic manager needs to be able to:

- call up an individual profile at will;
- focus in more detail on particular components;
- compare profiles, or individual components of profiles, of different institutions;
- aggregate components across institutions.

Operations of this nature are really only feasible if the information base is computerised. In this form it may also be used in conjunction with statistical packages which enable data to be analysed and modelled in increasingly sophisticated ways.

The components of a central information base should be determined after taking account of the needs of those involved in strategic management, and after consultation with staff in institutions. Much of the information and data which LEAs collect at present will find their way into the information base. In addition, other types of information, not collected by most LEAs in the past, will need to be included: information concerned with pupil attainment, curriculum organisation, customer perceptions and inspector judgements.

As has already been mentioned, a great deal of work has been carried out in recent years on the analysis of pupil attainments – especially in the form of public examination results – for use as measures of school performance. Gray *et al.* (1990), drawing on substantial research experience in the field, emphasise the importance of maintaining records on individual pupils and obtaining data on the prior attainments of pupils. They suggest that the development of pupil assessments in the context of the National Curriculum will potentially aid both concerns, and they urge LEAs to build suitable frameworks for the collection of the resultant data and their subsequent interpretation. They believe that LEAs need to consider ways in which to analyse and report their schools' results. The focus should be on the progress made by pupils and the schools' contribution, the so-called *added value* approach. Gray and his colleagues therefore argue that an LEA information base should include data on pupil attainment and have access to appropriate tools of statistical analysis.

Data bases on the secondary curriculum, both manual and computerised, have been in use in LEAs for several years. These have been particularly influenced by the curriculum analysis system developed by Wilcox and Eustace (1980). This system has been further developed in order to monitor nationally the pattern of the TVEI curriculum.

A quality management system is one 'designed to satisfy customer needs and expectations while serving to protect the company's interests' (BSI, 1987a). An educational institution or LEA which claims to operate a quality management system must therefore demonstrate a commitment to meeting customer needs. Such needs are not necessarily self-evident, and may only be discerned by actively seeking customer views. It is fair to say that current practices in education give considerably more attention to the views of the company – the school, the college or the LEA – than those of the customer – the pupil, the student, the parent and the potential employer. Actively seeking the views of the customer is therefore a *necessary* condition for any aspiration to recognition as a quality management system.

Although instruments have been designed to be used by individual colleges or schools (Theodossin and Thompson, 1987) they can be employed across institutions so as to achieve a comparative dimension. An example of the latter is provided by the A-Level Information System (ALIS) project based at the University of Newcastle which involves the participation of more than seventy schools and colleges in the LEAs of north east England (Hazelwood, 1990; Fitz-Gibbon, 1990). The ALIS project has *inter alia* been able to provide institutions with measures of their pupils' attitudes to particular A-level subjects, derived from a simple questionnaire. These measures can be compared with those obtained in other institutions. It would be entirely feasible for an LEA to sponsor a similar kind of exercise. A simple instrument, objectively and easily scored, could be developed to assess the general level of pupil/student satisfaction with particular aspects of school/college provision. This would be administered in each institution and the results sent to the LEA for collation and analysis. Information could be fed back to individual institutions in a form which would enable satisfaction levels to be compared with those in similar institutions.

Those who utilise the central information base may, of course, draw on other information and data. The aim is not to include everything about institutions but only that information which has demonstrable use. An officer or inspector concerned with a particular strategic management task would consult the information base as an initial starting point. In some cases it may contain sufficient information for the task in hand. It is more likely, however, that initial interrogation of the base will suggest ideas and possibilities requiring additional information. This may be obtained from other sources known and available to the enquirer. These could include books, journal articles and what has been referred to earlier as the informal information system.

An important additional source of information is contained within the information bases of individual institutions. A key principle of the information system described in chapter 4 is that detailed information should be retained at the institution level. The central information base should store only that which is necessary to fulfil the strategic management tasks of the LEA. When central planners require further information on an individual institution they will do what they have always done – they will get it from the institution concerned. Given the sophistication of computer technology this may increasingly be done from the centre by direct communication with the institutional information base.

What information should be held centrally and what at the institutional level? Who should have access to what and for what purposes? These questions reflect some of the key issues which must be addressed by those who seek to establish an information system of the kind proposed. Collaboration between the education department and institutions on these matters is essential if a system is to be established in which all can have confidence.

6

TIME-CONSTRAINED EVALUATION

THE NATURE OF TCE

An evaluation programme is composed of individual evaluations with four primary characteristics:

- *Utility*: an evaluation must have the prospect of being useful to some audience.
- *Feasibility*: an evaluation should be feasible in political, practical or cost effectiveness terms.
- *Propriety*: an evaluation should be conducted fairly and ethically.
- *Trustworthiness*: an evaluation should be carried out using methods which are regarded as appropriate and reliable by all concerned.

The characteristics are essentially those defined by the American *Joint Committee on Standards for Educational Evaluation* (Patton, 1987: 17–19).

Evaluations must, above all else, have utility. Evaluators are not involved in the pursuit of knowledge for its own sake. Evaluation should focus on and be driven by the information needs of the specific people who will use its findings. In an LEA these may include officers, committee members, a variety of institutional and programme managers, and teachers. In order to satisfy the multiple information requirements of many people, evaluations will often have to be swiftly carried out and reported on. In the absence of relevant information, decisions will be made as best they can. The repeated experience of information arriving too late or not at all reinforces the tendency towards crisis management.

112

Many of the practical evaluations required in LEAs, unlike those described in the academic literature, need to be conducted within very short time-scales. *Time-constrained evaluation* (TCE) is particularly relevant in the LEA context because of the large number of possible evaluands and the limited human and other resources available to meet them. If a comprehensive programme of evaluation is to be established, the time spent on most evaluations will be short. The evaluation of a major educational innovation may justify longer time spans but, even here, as the experience of TVEI shows, there will be a demand for regular feedback of findings throughout an evaluation.

An LEA is likely to be concerned with two broad groups of evaluation. There will be a small number of substantial evaluations conducted over a relatively protracted period ranging from a term to a year or more. These will tend, irrespective of their style – qualitative or quantitative, naturalistic or positivist – to resemble the forms of evaluation which are to be found in the academic research literature. Most evaluations will be concerned with the on-going information needs of the LEA. It is this group, where the time span is at most a matter of a few weeks, which merits the designation of time-constrained evaluation.

The full inspection provides the clearest example of TCE. As indicated earlier, the essential fieldwork processes involved – the collection and analysis of data, the formulation of provisional judgements and their feedback to staff – are effectively completed within a week. Other significant fieldwork activities of inspectors may be carried out within even shorter periods. Such substantially condensed periods of fieldwork may also be employed by those other than inspectors. For example, the staff of an institution conducting a self-evaluation will be involved in internal fieldwork which is typically of short duration.

The adoption of time-constrained approaches will be the characteristic of much of an LEA's programme of evaluation, particularly that provided by the activities of inspectors and staff within institutions. This is a necessary consequence of attempting to meet the utility criterion of evaluation. TCE also goes some way towards satisfying the criterion of feasibility. For example, in the particular form of inspection, TCE has high political salience for the government and all LEAs. It is, moreover, an approach which may appear eminently practical and understandable compared with the seemingly arcane practices of specialist evaluators. TCE, as carried out by inspectors and institutional staff, is also likely to be less costly than the alternative of employing external evaluators since, within any large organisation, it is carried out by its own personnel, often as part of other roles.

TCE is often carried out in LEAs and other large organisations without it being recognised as such. It occupies a somewhat obscure position between the familiar, ubiquitous and largely unexamined acts of making everyday judgements and the rarer, more discernible, high profile events of apparently greater objectivity meriting the description of research-style evaluation. The question is whether the practices underlying TCE, if brought to light, meet the criteria of propriety and trustworthiness. If not, can they be improved in order to do so? My aim will be to tackle these two issues by clarifying the general nature of TCE. This will mean identifying the stages involved in conducting a time-constrained evaluation and, more importantly, describing the general methods and procedures underlying them. Such a clarification, I believe, will be of help to a wide range of education and training staff – including national and local inspectorates – who are required, as at least part of their role, to commission and/or carry out monitoring and evaluation activities within short time spans.

TCE is essentially a *fieldwork* activity. In an educational or training context, the field is potentially all the arenas where learning or training, and the processes which support them, can occur. The notion of fieldwork implies a direct encounter with things as they are. It has its roots in anthropology and the social sciences generally. It is from these sources that the practice of TCE should draw. It is surprising that the fieldwork tradition is so weakly represented in both the rationale and practice of inspectorates. It is the lack of such a conceptual underpinning that may partly explain the ambiguity which some inspectors experience concerning their role, and the scepticism with which it is sometimes regarded by outsiders.

Although TCE needs to draw on fieldwork and social science traditions, it must not be supposed that the methods of the latter can simply be transferred to satisfy the requirements of the former. At the very least some adaptation will be necessary if they are to fit a specific context and the Procrustean bed

114

of limited time. From a conventional evaluation perspective, such adaptations would imply a loss of methodological rigour. Time-constrained evaluations might therefore be regarded as inferior versions of apparently more systematic and rigorous evaluations. Such a view, however, fails to take into account the fact that in any evaluation a trade-off inevitably occurs involving what may be seen as methodological rigour, the purposes of the evaluation and what can be realistically achieved in the given circumstances. Evaluation is justified in terms of its ability to generate information which is demonstrably useful to some individual, group or general audience. Information needs to be available when it is required. It is better to provide some information, even if it falls short of the ideals of comprehensiveness and quality, than none at all.

A more positive interpretation of TCE is to see it as a means of extending, systematising and refining the act of judgement. The nature of the relationship between judgement, information and action is often obscure. TCE seeks to clarify this relationship by providing information derived from known sources by clearly defined and acceptable methods specifically related to the user's needs. In brief, TCE is an attempt to make the processes by which information influences judgement and action both more visible and more truly professional.

CARRYING OUT AN EVALUATION

Figure 6.1 sets out a simple flowchart which identifies the main stages involved in carrying out an evaluation. The stages are essentially the same whether or not the evaluation is carried out under conditions of time-constraint. The extent of time-constraint influences the nature of the evaluation design chosen and the methods used for data collection, analysis and reporting, rather than the individual stages and their sequencing. The left hand side of the flowchart is concerned with *planning* an evaluation, and the right hand side with *carrying out* an evaluation. This chapter will be mainly concerned with the planning task and the pre-evaluation activity of meeting users and stakeholders, (1) to (6). The main stages in carrying out an evaluation, (7) to (10), are the subjects of the three subsequent chapters.

115

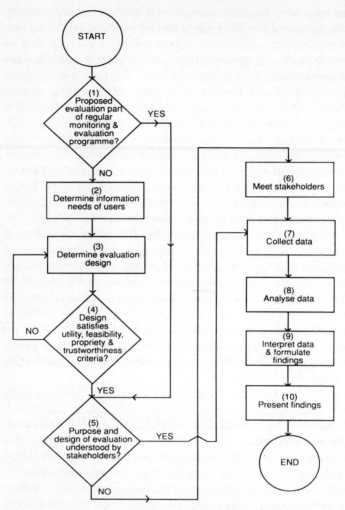

Figure 6.1 Planning and conducting an evaluation

The type of evaluation (1)

I have previously defined evaluation as a means of generating trustworthy information for use in strategic management at system level and unit level. The evaluations which are considered here are those that relate to strategic priorities and objectives. The starting point for any evaluation must therefore be with

116

the *use* and *users* of information. The use to which information will be put should be decided before conducting an evaluation and not afterwards. A major reason for the perceived lack of utility of much evaluation activity is the failure to follow this basic precept.

Information users (2)

Users require information to help with one or more of the following general categories of task: policy formulation and planning; organising programmes of advice, support and development; meeting accountability requirements; and informing the citizenry. In the case of a specific evaluation such broad descriptions of use are insufficiently precise to be very helpful. It is therefore necessary to engage the principal users in a discussion with the aim of identifying their specific information needs. The approach is close to the one recommended by Patton (1987) as *utilisation-focused evaluation*. Users are asked, for example: What difference would *that* information make? What would you do if you had an answer to *that* question? The outcome should be a series of tightly focused evaluation questions which have the commitment of users. Users would also indicate when the information is required for their purposes. The required speed of response will in part determine the extent to which any evaluation is time-constrained. The more clearly information needs and time-scales can be expressed, the better will be subsequent decisions concerning evaluation design and methods.

In some cases a single evaluation user exists. More typical, however, is the situation in which there are several users. For example, among the potential users of information produced from the evaluation of a TVEI project will be the local TVEI coordinator, LEA advisory staff, the heads and principals of the institutions involved and, perhaps more directly, the teaching staff associated with individual aspects of the TVEI curriculum. The task of consulting users and facilitating agreement on information needs is best carried out by the evaluator.

Users of information are an example of *stakeholders* in an evaluation. Another important stakeholder is the *client* or *sponsor*: those who initiate, authorise and legitimate evaluations. In most cases the sponsor will be the agent of the LEA or an institution.

Users and sponsors are separate roles, although occasionally they may be combined within a single person. For example, a head of a department in a school may ask staff to carry out a review of teaching and learning in their subject area. Here the head of department is the sponsor of the evaluation and also a likely user of the information produced. If the head of the department is actively involved in the review, as would seem probable, then the role of evaluator is also combined with those of sponsor and user.

In addition, an evaluation will often involve a number of stakeholders who will not be considered principal users of information. The conduct and outcomes of an institutional inspection, for example, will have implications for potentially all staff and not simply those managers who are expected to carry the main responsibility for responding to inspection findings and recommendations. Ideally all stakeholders would be involved in defining the information needs which evaluation should satisfy. Where the numbers are large, it may be necessary to restrict consultation to the principal users and/or a representative sample of stakeholders.

The possibility must be entertained of an occasional failure to identify information needs. This could arise because users do not see any need for additional information. It could be that users perceive their problems to be those of resourcing rather than information. However, even in this case, information may be useful on such matters as the type and level of resources needed, or how existing resources might be redeployed with greater effect. Much will depend on the evaluator's ability to interrogate users and to probe behind their first responses to questions about information needs. Where information needs cannot be adequately specified there is little to be gained by pressing on with an evaluation.

Determining the design of an evaluation (3) and (4)

Assuming that information needs can be specified, the next task of the evaluator will be to determine the design of the evaluation. The design is essentially an outline of how the evaluation is to be conducted. It attempts to answer a number of questions:

- *What is the purpose of the evaluation?*

This will be given in terms of the categories of information required by specific users.

- *Who is to carry out the evaluation?*
This may be a single evaluator or an evaluation team. Where a team of evaluators is involved it is usually necessary for one to have a major coordinating and leadership role. A team could also consist of both internal and external members. The decision on who is to be involved will depend on the level of human resources available.

- *What data will be used and how will it be collected?*
This is essentially a question about the methods of evaluation. In time-constrained evaluation three broad categories of method can be used based on: existing documentation and statistics; informal information systems; condensed fieldwork.

- *How will evaluators be used?*
This refers to the deployment of evaluators to particular aspects of the evaluation, the allocation of time to each, the methods to be used and the general scheduling of the evaluation as a whole.

- *How will the results be recorded and reported?*
This question relates to the problem of data analysis and interpretation. On this issue, particularly where naturalistic methods are involved, there is a general lack of consensus on an appropriate *modus operandi*. This question is addressed in chapter 9.

Involving stakeholders (5) and (6)

If at all possible, it is desirable for the principal users to be involved in the process of evaluation design. If users are to regard the findings of evaluation as helpful for their particular requirements, they will need to have confidence in the methods employed. The more an evaluator is able to talk through the rationale behind the methods employed, the more likely it is that the results of the evaluation will be owned by users.

Even where the utility criterion is met, it may still be the case that a proposed evaluation fails to satisfy stakeholders' views of feasibility, propriety and trustworthiness. If, after all reasonable efforts, stakeholders cannot be convinced that an evaluation will produce useful information by appropriate means then it should be discontinued.

If a viable design has been developed with the active knowledge and participation of all stakeholders, it may be possible to move straight away to the task of carrying out the evaluation. More often stakeholder involvement will have been partial or non-existent. It will therefore be necessary to communicate details of the proposed evaluation to stakeholders before the specific processes of data collection get under way. This is typically done through one or more pre-evaluation meetings.

The special case of inspection

In the case of a school inspection, the range of stakeholders includes the headteacher and staff, the governors, the parents, the local community and the LEA. Each of these will have somewhat different but overlapping informational needs, and expectations will therefore vary somewhat from group to group. The headteacher and staff are likely to be most interested in information which can help to facilitate the further development of the school. Governors will share this interest but may also see the inspection as a mechanism for expressing public accountability, as will the LEA. For parents and the community, an inspection potentially contributes to a general information service about educational provision locally. In addition, the LEA may expect the findings, along with those from similar inspections, to provide information useful for planning and policy formulation in the schools sector generally.

Typically, inspections do not attempt to identify the precise information needs appropriate to this range of general interests. Inspections tend to follow a predetermined pattern, perhaps with an implicit assumption that a variety of useful outcomes will naturally result. In most inspections the decisions corresponding to stages (2) to (5) in Figure 6.1 will have been taken in advance, mainly by inspectors and officers, with little involvement of the school and other stakeholders. The inspection process for most schools effectively begins at (6) with the pre-inspection visit.

As previously indicated, an inspection programme has to be planned well in advance and be tightly scheduled. It is therefore understandable that the objectives of inspections are often determined very largely by the inspectors as their collective enquiry unfolds. However, an effort made to ascertain the information needs of at least the headteacher and the senior staff could significantly improve the utility of the inspection from the school's point of view. This would not compromise the information agenda of the LEA. The aim should be to carry out an inspection which is demonstrably useful to both the school and the LEA.

PRE-EVALUATION PHASE

Stages (1) to (6) describe activities which take place before an evaluation begins. They constitute part of the pre-evaluation phase. In addition to these activities there are several others which are crucial to the success of the forthcoming evaluation. They are most conveniently carried out during initial visits made to the evaluand. These pre-evaluation visits need to be specifically programmed. For example, about eleven days are typically spent by a TSI on evaluating and producing a report on a youth training scheme. Of this total, two days will generally be allocated to pre-evaluation visits and other activities.

Apart from the desirability of involving stakeholders in determining the purposes and design of an evaluation, pre-evaluation visits may have the following aims:

- to enable evaluators to gain access to and establish trust with stakeholders;
- to facilitate stakeholders' understanding and acceptance of the conduct of evaluation;
- to collect background information and documentation on the evaluand in order to increase the evaluators' understanding of the evaluand;
- to negotiate a provisional timetable for the evaluation and the necessary domestic and other support which the evaluators will require while on site.

Access and trust

The mere fact that an evaluation has a sponsor does not guarantee that the evaluator will have no problems in gaining access to stakeholders. The cooperation of stakeholders has to be won even where they are managerially subordinate to the sponsor. A common assumption of evaluators and policy makers is that evaluations do not have the characteristics of other social situations. They assume, naïvely, that all parties involved in an evaluation will suspend any vested interests and accord it special status (Noblit and Eaker, 1988). Teachers, for example, who have been committed by their headteacher to participate in an evaluation – even a self-evaluation – may decide to what extent it is in their interests to be forthcoming to the probings of an evaluator. Other stakeholders and potential respondents may not be under the managerial jurisdiction of the sponsor. Thus, although approval may be given for an evaluator to approach parents, their active participation in an evaluation cannot be compelled. An evaluator has to be prepared to negotiate access with each new group of stakeholders.

A necessary condition for gaining access and getting established is building trust. Respondents are more likely to be open and forthcoming if they have trust in the evaluator's integrity. The difficulties of establishing trust are compounded where more than one evaluator is involved. Each evaluator has to win trust anew with every potential respondent encountered. The chain of trust can therefore be broken at any point by the actions of any individual.

Gaining trust and establishing good working relationships are particularly at risk where time is at a premium as in time-constrained evaluation. A permanent team of inspectors has some advantage in this regard over individual investigators appointed to one-off evaluations. Inspectors have an opportunity to establish a reputation for integrity in their LEA as a result of the repeated and successful practice of inspection over a period of time. A permanent team is also more likely to have the time together to develop the social skills and self-awareness needed to encourage productive working relationships with school and college staff.

The conduct of evaluation

Although the personal skills of the evaluator are important, they are insufficient by themselves to ensure the existence of a climate of trust within which an evaluation can take place.

Those who are to be involved in an evaluation also need to have confidence in the way in which the evaluation will be conducted. This requires an understanding and acceptance of both the methodological and ethical principles on which an evaluation is premised. The two sets of principles are not of course totally independent. A methodology is ultimately based on value assumptions and thus encapsulates certain ethical principles. However, since these often go unrecognised it is worth while making the distinction and treating the ethical concerns separately from those of methodology. An evaluator needs to be able to communicate clearly to stakeholders, both individually and collectively, the approach to be used in a particular evaluation. It will be an advantage if the evaluator has the approach briefly documented so that all potential stakeholders have access to a copy.

As far as methodology is concerned the description should cover such matters as the kind of data which will be collected and by what means. Some indication of the methods of data analysis to be used, and how results will be obtained and presented, should be included. An inspectorate which is in the position of carrying out evaluations on a regular basis will find it useful to have a short and easily produced document available covering the range of its approaches. The DES (1986a) series *Reporting Inspections*, describing the methods used by HMI in different educational sectors, provides an example of the kind of document, capable of mass circulation, which is envisaged.

As implied above, evaluation is neither a value-neutral nor an emotion-free activity. In the particular form of inspection it has tended to be viewed by teachers in an anxious if not hostile light. Evaluations carried out by LEA inspectors have the potential of being more threatening to teachers than those of HMI. HMI, after all, has no direct bearing on the careers of individual teachers. LEA inspectors are fairly permanent local figures and have opportunities to influence preferment. For these reasons and others it is important that evaluation, whether carried out by inspectors or by those within an institution, has an agreed code of ethics established to govern its practice. Otherwise there is a very real danger that evaluation could become a crude apparatus of teacher surveillance and tyranny.

An embryonic ethical code is apparent in the practice of

HMI and some LEA inspectorates. This is captured in such maxims as:

- Inspect the teaching not the teachers.
- Do good as you go.
- Do not say anything to a headteacher which has not already been said in greater detail to the teachers concerned.
- An inspection report when published should contain no surprises.

In the final section of this chapter I set out some possible principles for an ethical code relevant to the special case of time-constrained evaluation.

Background information

It is often the case that an evaluator will not know much about a particular evaluand prior to the decision to evaluate it. In a time-constrained evaluation it is essential that the evaluator gathers as much background as possible before the exercise begins. This will enable the evaluator to formulate a provisional model of the evaluand. Making the model explicit by setting it out on paper can be a useful exercise. Often it is not until an idea is committed to paper that its full possibilities become apparent. Doing so may also lead to the recognition that the notional model does not stand up to scrutiny. This may in turn mean recourse to a more satisfactory version. At the very least, setting out the model may be a convenient way of summarising a mass of detail and thus minimising the burden on the memory. The model – derived as it will be from limited data – will be incomplete. Its success depends on its ability to generate questions which the evaluator will want to explore when in the field. The model provides an initial means of organising the evaluator's thinking and getting the enquiry under way. As evidence is collected and assessed it will necessarily be revised. By the end of the evaluation, it will have undergone substantial modification.

In an institutional inspection the provisional model may be provided by means of a summary of the background documentation prepared by the Reporting Inspector for the benefit of all members of the inspection team. The RI may also include other information acquired during the pre-inspection visit through discussions with institution staff and initial observation. Such a summary is an invaluable aid in getting a team of inspectors to a comparable level of understanding about the institution, and ensuring that they can begin their enquiries with minimal delay.

A pre-evaluation visit will also enable the evaluator to negotiate the details of the timetable for the evaluation and the arrangements needed to support it. The latter will involve identifying: the individuals who are to participate in the evaluation; the procedures to be followed for making contact with them; any facilities required; and such domestic arrangements as the provision of refreshments. Where an evaluation team is involved these kinds of logistical arrangements can be quite complex.

ETHICAL ISSUES

Evaluation is concerned with the generation of information and knowledge, the use of which may influence the development of institutions and programmes, and thereby the individuals involved in them. In so far as evaluation involves and affects individuals, it is inevitably concerned with ethical issues. In recent years, the question of ethics has been a concern particularly of those evaluators using case-study approaches (see Simons, 1987). Surprisingly, little attention seems to have been given to these matters by those outside the community of academic evaluators. Although ethical principles may be considered to be implicit in the practice of inspection, no explicit ethical code seems to have been formulated. The ethical dimension has also not figured significantly in the post-ERA developments of LEA evaluation.

A basic principle which typically informs ethical codes established to regulate the conduct of research in the social sciences is that of *fully informed consent*. The notion of consent is applicable where people voluntarily take part in a research or evaluation study. It is not appropriate in a situation, for example, where teachers are involved in an institutional evaluation authorised by the LEA, since it has statutory powers under the 1944 Education Act to carry out inspections of its schools. Teachers cannot therefore refuse to take part in inspections. Teachers are also required, under their conditions of employment, to participate in any internal inspection required by their headteacher.

In the case of LEA- or institution-sponsored evaluations, a more appropriate principle might be described as *fully informed participation*. This principle balances the requirement for participation with the obligation, on the evaluator's part, of ensuring that those involved are fully informed about what the evaluation entails. This should be taken to mean that individuals are guaranteed to know what the purposes of the evaluation are, what is expected of them, the methods to be employed in conducting the evaluation and how the findings will be presented. Where few individuals are involved, the information may be provided orally in one-to-one situations. Where numbers are larger, it will be necessary to prepare a brief written outline which can be circulated to all concerned or to meet the staff as a group.

Communicating details in these ways is important. Evaluations tend to raise anxieties among those involved, and misunderstandings and suspicions can often occur. For example, in institutional evaluations involving classroom observation, teachers often assume that the process is equivalent to teacher appraisal. It is therefore important to make it clear that institutional evaluation and teacher appraisal are two distinct processes (Poster and Poster, 1991). In the former case the aim is not to describe individual teachers but rather the total teaching and learning experience.

This leads us to a consideration of a second general principle which underlies ethical codes in the social sciences: the *individual's right to privacy*. The application of this principle has to be set against the potentially competing one of the *public's right to know*. Striking the right balance between the two is difficult, particularly at a time when accountability concerns are in the ascendant. One way of attempting to reconcile the two principles is to ensure that the descriptive outcomes of evaluations are written to provide a general rather than a person-specific account. Thus, a description of the approaches to teaching and learning in a geography department is appropriate whereas an account of the styles and methods of individual teachers is not. It should be said, however, that there can be no absolute guarantee of anonymity.

General descriptions of aspects of an institution will often be developed from a series of observations made of individuals in specific contexts. The description of the geography department will have been derived *inter alia* from observations made of individual geography teachers with specific pupil groups. The evaluator will have some kind of record of these individual sessions, each of which in part constitutes a description of the teaching approach of one individual. Such records may be shared with the individuals concerned but would not normally be made available to others in the institution. Given the anxiety felt by teachers on this issue it is important to maintain the sharp distinction between information generated for institution or programme evaluation and that for appraisal purposes.

In the case of inspection, the notes on individual contexts may be aggregated in order to contribute to an LEA-wide picture. Thus a geography inspector may use the notes made on individual but anonymous geography lessons during inspections in order to build up an understanding of trends and practices in geography teaching in schools generally. The establishment of such an information base would be an invaluable resource in planning central programmes of curriculum and in-service training support in geography.

Where anxieties of being individually appraised can be assuaged, teachers may still require reassurance that the evaluation of a lesson takes proper account of the context and relevant antecedents. In other words, teachers will want to be confident that appropriate assessments of individual lessons are made even where they recognise that these eventually contribute to general rather than teacher-specific accounts. This concern may often be expressed as a wish by teachers to know the criteria on which judgements are to be made. Evaluators need to make explicit and communicate these clearly to those involved in an evaluation.

Two important provisos need to be stated. First, criteria act as a general framework for evaluation. There are no criteria which can be applied mechanically to every situation. No sound judgement can be made about what is appropriate in an individual lesson unless the evaluator is able to relate the lesson to:

- its place in the sequence of lessons as determined by the teacher;
- the facilities and materials to which the teacher has access;
- the nature of the learners;
- and what the teacher intended to achieve in the lesson.

It is *wrong* to make a judgement which implicates another

human being on the basis of a partial understanding of the situation. The minimum requirement is that, in every lesson observed, the teacher's perception of what took place is sought.

The second proviso is that, even if criteria are made explicit and other supporting evidence is at hand, there is no neat calculus available which is able to weigh the pros and the cons and thus arrive at an unambiguous and totally objective assessment of a lesson. In the final analysis, there are no routine procedures that can be employed to absolve one from making a judgement. This is because education is at heart a value-contested undertaking. Educational entities are social constructions which seek to make sense of certain aspects of our shared experience. The evaluator's task is to identify the constructions of others and to relate them to their own in order to generate new constructions which are more meaningful and more consensual.

If the view of the evaluator outlined in the previous paragraph is generally acceptable, then an important question must be: Whose constructions should be sought? In the evaluation of a single lesson the teacher, who has most to lose or gain from any outcome, is undoubtedly the principal stakeholder. But what of the pupils? Should their view of the lesson be sought as well as that of the teacher? If so, should this be done by asking pupils to complete some kind of questionnaire? If this were done by the teacher alone, unprompted by any external evaluator, then pupils might perceive the exercise to be a serious and sincere attempt to understand and respond to their needs. It might enhance their esteem for the teacher. If, however, the questionnaire were administered by the evaluator then it is likely that pupils would perceive the situation differently and, more importantly, their regard for the teacher might be lessened. This kind of issue is related to another frequently invoked ethical principle – *protection from harm*. If the professional esteem in which a teacher was held by pupils or peers were diminished as a result of the actions of an evaluator then the situation might be described as one of psychological harm.

All that has been said applies equally to other aspects of institutional evaluation. Assessment of the effectiveness of management arrangements is increasingly becoming a signifi-cant feature of the inspection of schools and colleges by HMI.

Key stakeholders in this regard are the headteacher/principal and senior staff. By its very nature management is much more difficult than teaching to observe in action. It has to be assessed indirectly, very often by looking for its effects or by talking to members of the senior management team. The purpose of good management is *inter alia* to create the proper environment and facilities to enable teachers to do their job; and to ignore the perspective of teachers – the other major stakeholder group – is likely to result in a partial assessment. The commitment to involving several stakeholder groups, where appropriate, has the additional benefit of helping to ensure that an evaluation is not solely based, as can sometimes be the case, on the perspectives of those with the most power. We have here perhaps an approximation to a further principle, reflecting commitment to democratic ideals, of *valuing the constructions of different stakeholder groups equally*.

Conducting a style of evaluation which respects multiple perspectives and multiple information sources while aiming at the development of consensual constructions is not easy. Moreover, the approach poses particular problems under conditions of time-constraint. In these circumstances evaluators have to utilise as much available information as possible in the short time at their disposal. This may mean rethinking the usual stance on confidentiality, so that any relevant information from discussions, conversations or meetings is counted as being on the record unless there is a specific request to regard such sources as confidential.

The procedures that might be used in progressively checking out emerging consensual constructions with representatives of stakeholder groups inevitably become attenuated when time spans are short. Much has to be done in the evaluator's head and notebook during the course of the evaluation. The main consensual check may be done towards the end of the evaluation when constructions are fed back orally at a meeting of stakeholders. Ideally there would be a further opportunity, as soon as possible thereafter, for a more systematic scrutiny of proposed constructions using the initial draft of the evaluation report. The evaluator has the obligation to consider suggestions from stakeholders which seek to: correct perceived inaccuracies; add further information for the purposes of increasing clarity; reject proposed constructions or replace them with others. The evaluator also has the obligation to indicate the nature of the information used in framing any construction, whether descriptive or evaluative, when challenged to do so. Evaluators, however, are not obliged to change their reports if, after having given due regard to stakeholders' suggestions, they remain unconvinced of their merit. In such cases, stakeholders should have the right to submit their disagreements in writing and for these to be included as an appendix to the final version of the report.

7

DATA COLLECTION AND ANALYSIS: 1

INTRODUCTION

The previous two chapters were concerned with the organisation of a system-wide evaluation programme. The individual components making up such a programme have been described as falling into one of two groups: research-style evaluation; or time-constrained evaluation. The latter is likely to be the more widely used and forms the subject of this chapter and the one to follow.

The purpose of evaluation is to generate information for users. Such information is in turn derived from data, the relatively discrete and separate pieces of information which are subsequently transformed into larger, more inclusive and more meaningful components. Data may be obtained in various qualitative and quantitative forms: verbal, numerical, symbolic, even pictorial.

The three main categories of data collection referred to in the previous chapter involve methods based on: existing records and documents; informal information systems; condensed fieldwork. For the purposes of clarity I shall deal with each of these separately, although any particular evaluation may in fact use methods associated with any two or all of the categories. The first two will be the subject of this chapter, the third will be dealt with in the next.

The first two categories of method remind us that, when faced with the task of carrying out an evaluation, the information we need may already be available. In some cases the information may be extracted and used directly. More often, existing information will require reworking – even quite substantial transformation – in order to illuminate issues other than those for which it was originally collected.

The formal information system consists of all the statistics, records and documents that any organisation maintains, usually in a multiplicity of individual and corporate files, manual and computerised. To avoid information being collected that was already available within the organisation, an *inventory* should be maintained of all the types of information that are collected on a regular basis. Such an inventory should be freely available to all within the organisation, and might list: type of information; format of the information; method of storage; principal collector; frequency of collection; uses of the information; how and where it can be accessed.

The informal information system may be regarded as consisting of individual informal information bases, one for each member of the information community. Each informal information base is in a dynamic relationship with the formal information system. Content from one may pass to the other allowing the content of individual informal information bases to be shared and combined, yielding new information and knowledge. This process will take place naturally – although often unsystematically – through conversation, discussions and meetings.

This chapter will examine some structured methods of exploiting existing information, in both the formal and informal information systems, for the purposes of time-constrained evaluation.

USE OF RECORDS AND DOCUMENTS

This section is concerned with the evaluative potential of a variety of *official* documentation that exists at system and unit levels. Guba and Lincoln (1981) make a distinction between records and documents. A record may be defined as:

> any written statement prepared by an individual or agency for the purpose of attesting to an event or providing an accounting . . . [Records] form an official chronicle that is part of a larger work, usually on the processes and proceedings of public affairs.
>
> (Guba and Lincoln, 1981: 228)

In contrast, a *document*:

> serve[s] to make others aware of a point of view, to persuade, to aggrandise, to explicate, or to justify.
>
> (Guba and Lincoln, 1981: 230)

Two things are immediately apparent. First, the amount of official documentation which exists, even within a small school, is very substantial. Second, this type of documentation is very rarely used for purposes beyond those for which it was originally intended. In particular, it has been almost totally neglected as a source of evaluative data and information. The time-constrained evaluator should consider using existing documentation wherever possible.

The use of such documents and records has other advantages. They will generally be available on a low- or no-cost basis. In particular:

> both documents and records represent a 'natural' source of information. Not only are they, in fact, an 'in context' source of information – that is, they arise from the context and exist in it – but they consist of information about the context. Records show what happened in the context, and documents record a variety of other evidence about the environment and people's perceptions of it. They are thus repositories of well-grounded data on the events or situations under investigation.
>
> (Guba and Lincoln, 1981: 232)

They are also *non-reactive*, that is, the subjects of documents or records do not influence and are not influenced by the evaluator.

The mere fact of availability is no guarantee that official documents may be valid sources for evaluative purposes. The status of each document and record needs to be assessed. This may be done using questions such as these as a possible framework for assessment:

- Who was the author of the document or the compiler of the record?
- What was the purpose of the author/compiler?
- For whom was the document written or the record compiled?
- On what sources of information did the author/compiler draw?

- From what standpoint or perspective is the document written or record compiled?
- Is the document or record available in the form as originally written or compiled? Has it been edited, reduced or adjusted in any way? Is the original version available?
- To what extent are the professional and other interests of the author/compiler served by the document or record? What is the nature and likely extent of any bias thereby introduced?
- Is there any other documentation available that might corroborate or extend the content of the document or record under consideration?

Answers to these questions may occasionally raise doubts about the reliability of documentation. Where records are concerned it may sometimes be possible to test such matters as accuracy by carrying out a spot check on a sample. Documents, however, are much more difficult to validate. Usually it will be possible to indicate the degree of reliability which can be placed on source documentation only by pointing out to a potential reader the extent of any limitations revealed.

Content analysis

Even where there is confidence in source documentation, there is still the necessity to show that the methods used in transforming it to yield evaluative information are broadly acceptable. One such method is *content analysis* defined as: 'any technique for making inferences by objectively and systematically identifying specified characteristics of messages' (Holsti, 1969: 14).

A key process is that of categorisation. Guba and Lincoln (1981) suggest that good categories should: reflect the purposes of the research; be exhaustive, mutually exclusive and independent; be derived from a single classification principle. They suggest, however, that the construction of categories is often a trial-and-error process forcing the analyst to move between the data and an *a priori* or grounded theory. Categories are modified until the process is complete with each datum sensibly accounted for. The aim should be to describe the process of categorisation employed in terms of a series of rules and criteria such that an independent analyst could apply them to the same material and arrive at the same results.

Content analysis can be carried out on single or multiple documents. Figure 7.1 shows an example of the latter. This summarises part of a study carried out a number of years ago in response to a request for information concerning the provision of religious education in an LEA's secondary schools. A study was mounted using existing documentation.

SYLLABUS TOPICS	Year 7	Year 8	Year 9	Year 10	Year 11
OLD TESTAMENT STUDIES	11	13	5	2	1
GOSPEL STUDIES	8	20	13	6	5
ACTS OF THE APOSTLES		2	4	1	
BIBLE AS A BOOK	6	3		2	1
BACKGROUND TO THE BIBLE	2	2	4	1	
HISTORY OF THE CHRISTIAN CHURCH		1	7	1	
GREAT CHRISTIANS	1	4	6	2	2
CHRISTIAN SECTS & DENOMINATIONS	1	2	3	1	
SOCIETY & RELIGION/ CHRISTIANITY	3	3	7	19	20
PERSONAL PROBLEMS & CHRISTIANITY	2		4	17	18
COMPARATIVE RELIGION	3	2	8	7	9
NATURE OF RELIGION	1	1	1	1	3
THE EXTERNALS OF RELIGION	3	4	1		
BELIEFS OF PRIMITIVE PEOPLE	1				
DEATH AND LIFE			1		
WORLD VIEWS OTHER THAN RELIGIOUS			1		
PRACTICAL COMMUNITY SERVICE				2	2

Figure 7.1 Example of a content analysis of R.E. syllabuses of 32 schools

The figure is a content analysis of the syllabuses of 32 secondary schools. The syllabuses were of varying lengths, formats and styles. In brief, the procedure of analysis adopted involved several operations. The syllabuses were read through to get an impression of their scope and treatment. This resulted in a provisional set of general topic categories. These were applied to a sample of the syllabuses and adjusted until all of the content could be located comfortably within them. The category system was then used on the complete set of syllabuses. This in turn required minor adjustment to the number and designation of the categories. Each category was defined in terms of a brief explanatory paragraph. Each syllabus was then examined in turn, and up to four categories were identified, representing the major discrete emphases within each year group, that is, those which did not arise incidentally out of the teaching of aspects covered by other topics.

The example illustrates the valuable use of time-constrained methods of enquiry by an LEA. Requests for information and for studies to be carried out are a frequent occurrence in LEAs, with time to meet them always at a premium. Education committee members tend to expect results of an enquiry at their next meeting, and inspectors and officers seldom have the luxury of a protracted period to pursue a particular issue or enquiry in a single-minded fashion. The reality is that senior staff in an LEA education department are typically dealing with several major concerns simultaneously. As inspectors are called upon to evaluate adherence to the National Curriculum as part of accountability procedures, syllabus content analysis will become increasingly important.

The case aggregation method

Guba and Lincoln (1981) distinguish between documents of two types: those which are broadly similar to each other and where content analysis may be appropriately used, and those which have different formats, organisation or content categories and deal with different instances of the same or like phenomenon. A particular example is where the documents are case studies of similar programmes, projects or institutions which require aggregation or integration under a common conceptual framework. This is a situation increasingly encountered in multi-site innovation projects where the aim is to isolate common themes and issues (see Ebbutt, 1988).

The problems involved are well illustrated in the national evaluation of pilot schemes of Records of Achievement (Broadfoot *et al.*, 1988). Case studies were carried out by the evaluation team on twenty-one schools and one tertiary college. In addition, reports were available from the project directors and, in some cases, the local evaluators of each of the nine pilot schemes from which the twenty-two institutions were drawn. The former were used to generate an *across-site* analysis and the latter an *across-scheme* analysis. The framework for both analyses derived from the criteria and issues identified from the 1984 DES statement of policy on Records of Achievement. As the evaluation progressed, other themes and issues emerged which were added to the list. The framework for analysis was progressively developed and refined in an iterative process of dialogue with participants in the evaluation, achieved mainly through the vehicle of a series of interim reports produced by the team.

Compiling the cross-scheme analysis from the reports of project directors proved to be particularly difficult because of marked differences in style and the inevitable selectivity of project directors in the detail of the issues they addressed. As a consequence, no attempt was made to pass judgement on particular schemes, or to compare and contrast their effectiveness. What was finally reported was a summary and analysis of the schemes as perceived by the project directors. This was useful since, compared with the cross-site analysis, greater prominence was given to management and other matters that went beyond the school.

The evaluators claimed that the analysis they used in their cross-site study came close to the *constant comparative method* described by Glaser and Strauss (1967). Indeed this method is especially applicable where analytical categories emerge from the data rather than being derived from an *a priori* theory or model.

The analysis of records

Records are an essential means by which an organisation attempts to keep track of what is going on. When new initiatives are taken, existing records may be modified or extended, or a new record system established. In principle, the effects of any activity or event occurring within an organisation may be discerned either directly or indirectly in the entries made in its system of records. Requests for information arise all the time in every organisation. Often these can be responded to by individuals directly or after minimal consultation with appropriate colleagues. Sometimes, however, a more extensive exercise is required, involving a systematic scrutiny of existing records. This will be particularly so where information of an evaluative nature is sought. Although some initiatives may be systematically evaluated, this is by no means always the case. Moreover, planned evaluations are more likely to be associated with relatively few new initiatives rather than with a larger number of on-going developments. Frequently the examination of existing records may be the only feasible means of obtaining information quickly on issues of current concern.

An illustration will be helpful here. A governing body of a secondary school asks the headteacher to report at its next meeting on the effects of the introduction two years previously of an integrated science course. What information is available from existing records which can be used in compiling a report which will in effect be a retrospective evaluation of the course?

The head of department recalls that there had been regular reporting on progress at departmental meetings. An analysis of the minutes picks up staff perceptions of any benefits attributable to the new course or any problems or difficulties associated with it. Book withdrawal records of the school library are scrutinised for evidence of any enhanced interest in science. Science club records are examined to see whether there was any indication of increased interest and membership as a result of the new course. Post-GCSE take-up of science courses is compared with that of other subjects and previous years.

Records can be of two broad types – concerned either with individuals or with institutions and programmes. Those of the first type are more familiar. In schools and colleges the records of pupils/students constitute a major group. Typically such records have been used only to evaluate the performance of individuals. When suitably aggregated they may also be used in the evaluation of institutions and programmes. It is in this latter capacity that they are of interest to our concerns here. Most use has been made of the public examination results of pupils in Years 11–13. For an individual school, pupil results may be aggregated for each subject so that performance can be monitored from year to year and the effects of any major interventions, for example, a new curriculum initiative, assessed. This assumes that pupil ability remains constant from year to year. While this may be true for the intake to a school as a whole it will not necessarily be so for the particular pupil samples that take individual subjects. If scores on one or more relevant standardised tests are available, then the examination results actually obtained can be adjusted statistically to account for any significant variations from one year to another in intake ability. Examination results are also frequently aggregated to monitor performance across a whole LEA and to compare the effectiveness of one school with another. As already noted, the latter requires particular care in allowing for differences in pupil ability from school to school.

The potential for aggregating other pupil characteristics for monitoring and evaluation purposes has generally been much neglected at both institutional and LEA levels. For example, few schools have utilised the data contained in pupil registers to reveal on a regular basis the aggregated attendance of pupils analysed by such factors as form group, gender, day of the week and so on.

Institutional records: an example

Just as records may detail the characteristics of individual pupils so too they may set out the features of individual institutions or programmes. Institutional records often take the form of specific *returns* collected by LEAs or the DES. In recent years many LEAs have required a curriculum return. This typically records the details of the organisation of the school curriculum according to year and form groups. The Sheffield curriculum return for secondary schools (Wilcox and Eustace, 1980) has been adopted by a number of LEAs. Such returns provide an LEA with a valuable curriculum information base. The information can be reworked in a variety of ingenious ways to generate indicators which enable

139

patterns of curriculum organisation to be monitored on an LEA-wide basis.

An example is provided in Figure 7.2 which summarises the pattern of mixed ability organisation as it was in the secondary schools of an LEA some years ago. The results are analysed by school and year group in terms of an indicator of mixed ability. The indicator has values ranging from 0 to 1.

The indicator was computed from two basic components which could easily be extracted from the curriculum returns. The first was the proportion of pupils in a particular year group present in the largest ability band or stream. The larger the number of bands or streams the smaller the proportion defined above will be. The minimum value of 0 may be approached but not reached. If the year group was not banded or streamed the component has the maximum value of 1. If a year group of 150 pupils has 33 pupils in the largest band or stream, the value of the component is $33/150 = 0.22$.

The second component is the proportion of the timetable for which pupils in the largest band or stream are present in teaching groups which have not been further constituted on the basis of ability. The maximum value of 1 corresponds to the absence of further ability segregation within the band or year group. The minimum value of 0 describes the situation where the teaching groups in all subjects have been determined on the basis of ability. Values of this component will therefore range from 0 to 1. Thus a band or year group which has 10 out of the 40 periods per week regrouped on the basis of ability sets will have a value of $40-10 = 30/40 = 0.75$.

When values for the two components are multiplied together they produce the overall mixed ability indicator. Values of the indicator approaching 0 correspond to year groups with fine ability grouping. Values approaching 1 represent year groups where ability grouping is much less evident. Attainment of the maximum value of 1 corresponds to pure mixed ability grouping.

The use of performance indicators

The above example acts as a reminder that the notion of existing documentation needs to be extended to include information which is available in a quantitative form. PIs represent one

Mixed ability rating for each year group

School	Year 7	Year 8	Year 9	Year 10	Year 11
1	0.65	0.65	0.48	0.50	0.30
2		0.88	0.58	0.55	0.45
3		0.73	0.65	0.90	0.90
4	1.00	0.46	0.44	0.38	0.31
5	1.00	0.75	0.75	0.88	0.88
6	0.51	0.59	0.51	0.43	0.41
7	0.91	0.73	0.73	0.76	0.56
8		0.32	0.36	0.04	0.26
9	1.00	1.00			
10		0.70	0.36	0.66	0.64
11	0.86	0.51	0.63	0.20	0.20
12	0.50	0.39	0.27	0.25	0.30
13		0.91	0.64	0.73	0.56
14	1.00	0.88	0.73	0.88	0.88
15	0.28	0.47	0.42	0.43	0.40
16	0.28	0.27	0.47	0.23	0.19
17		0.25	0.22	0.03	0.04
18		0.83	0.45	0.31	0.34
19	1.00	1.00	1.00	1.00	1.00
20	0.43	0.44	0.45	0.58	0.60
21	1.00	0.64	0.42	0.25	0.35
22	1.00	0.70	0.75	0.60	0.70
23	0.53	0.21	0.17	0.39	0.43
24	1.00	0.33	0.42	0.24	0.31
25		0.78	0.62	0.87	0.87
26		0.31	0.35	0.30	0.39
27	0.49	0.51	0.52	0.34	0.35
28	1.00	0.85	0.85	0.80	0.80
29	0.79	0.56	0.47	0.88	0.88
30	0.37	0.38	0.35	0.39	0.32
31	0.58	0.34	0.26	0.19	0.17
32	1.00	1.00	0.44	0.47	0.51
33	1.00	0.43	0.40	0.53	0.32
34	0.88	0.81	0.54	1.00	1.00
35	1.00	1.00	1.00	0.54	0.51
36	0.56	0.60	0.37	0.43	0.41
37		0.75	0.75	0.52	0.51
38	0.51	0.48	0.43	0.35	0.45
39	1.00	0.88	0.88	0.88	0.88

Figure 7.2 Example of a curriculum return analysis

current manifestation of the latter. There has been a significant upsurge of interest in PIs of late and a number of developments are under way. It is to be expected that in due course comprehensive PI systems will be available at programme, institution and system levels. At present, however, there is little experience of their use for monitoring and evaluation purposes.

A promising indication of what the future might hold in store is provided by the A-Level Information System (ALIS) project (Fitz-Gibbon, 1990). The ALIS team collects information from the participating institutions and produces short reports which deal with A-level examination results, students' attitudes to their institution and the A-level subjects they study, and teaching processes and contexts. Confidentiality is maintained by having all the data reported under code names chosen by each institution. The staff at each school or college can see their own data in the context of those from other institutions, without being able to identify the names of the other institutions. The reports present the data in the form of PIs. These effectively provide heads of institutions and subject departments with evaluative information relevant to the following kinds of questions:

- Were the A-level results in line with expectations?
- Did students have a positive attitude to the A-level subjects studied?
- Were students participating in a broad variety of extra-curricular activities?
- Did the students have a positive attitude to the school or college?
- Were students' aspirations in line with their abilities and achievements?

(See Fitz-Gibbon, 1990: 89)

Of course, the production of an indicator system of this scope is not a time-constrained activity. It is a substantial enterprise which involves considerable time and resourcing. The costs of the system, including the appointment of a full-time project worker, are borne by the participating LEAs. However, the point of referring to the system here is to emphasise that the results which are produced enable others to engage in time-constrained evaluative enquiry. This might be done within a school by convening a meeting of staff to consider the results relevant to their subject department, leading to the production of a short report outlining the implications for the further development of the subject concerned. Such an exercise might easily be completed for a total time cost of one hour for each member of the department and a further three hours for a rapporteur to produce the report.

Once a PI system has been established it will need continued resourcing so that it can be maintained permanently. PIs will be required on a regular basis, at least annually. Once PIs are produced on a predictable and easily accessible basis they are likely to be used by a wide range of staff for a variety of purposes. One of these purposes is to provide the basic data on which to carry out time-constrained enquiry.

Documentation: an evaluation resource

I have been at pains to stress here that existing documentation forms a rather neglected evaluation resource. The amount of information which is potentially available to the evaluator is considerable, and can include simple numerical data, statistics of one kind or another – performance indicators, records and documents of different length, format and complexity. There are some evaluative enquiries which can adequately be carried out using documentation alone. In many cases that may be done sufficiently rigorously to justify the title of an evaluation. Where it is also done swiftly, it constitutes a form of time-constrained evaluation. How, it might be asked, does the latter differ from the familiar activity of summarising the contents of written materials? To count as an evaluation an exercise must be carried out by applying a systematic method which is open to scrutiny. In addition, where multiple documentation is concerned, the aim is not simply to produce a summary but to generate new understandings. One of the problems is that at present the methods of analysing complex documentation are not well established. This is a characteristic of the analysis of qualitative data in general and is an issue which is considered in more detail in the chapter which follows.

In an evaluative enquiry, documentation is often used together with other sources of data. This is apparent in the practice of inspection. For example, as already outlined in the previous chapter, a key feature is the collection and interpretation of background information and documentation relevant to the institution or programme to be inspected. Another example of the use of documentation during an inspection is the common practice of examining the work produced by pupils. This is typically done by collecting a sample of the work representing pupils of different ability levels. The work is then scrutinised by one or more inspectors at convenient points during the actual inspection. Where several inspectors are involved, comments and views are fed back to a lead inspector who is responsible for producing an overview. This will then be checked out with the other inspectors in a team meeting, usually during the period of the inspection. A major purpose of the exercise is to get an understanding of the quality of pupils' work, and its development over time. It is a potentially useful complement to the impressions gained through the 'snapshots' made during visits to the classroom. It provides a striking example of a complex evaluative task carried out under conditions of extreme time-constraint.

USE OF THE INFORMAL INFORMATION SYSTEM

Each of us carries around in our heads a vast amount of information and knowledge about the world. Part of that informal information base is concerned with matters relating to our job or profession. As an educationist I have available a store of information related to specific subjects, methods of teaching and learning, particular students and educational institutions, educational theories and much more besides. I also have ways of making sense of new educational situations in which I find myself. Thus, if I go to a school I have not visited before my existing knowledge and general ways of thinking and observing will enable me to come to some kind of understanding of what goes on inside it. If someone asks me about a particular school or educational programme I may be able to provide an appropriate description in some detail. If I am asked about certain educational developments I am able to offer an assessment of their respective merits. I may find myself with a group of colleagues in a situation where we attempt to pool our knowledge on current developments in primary schools. In doing so, we may find that we are able to interpret what was going on in terms of certain provisional hypotheses, which previously we had not made explicit.

In other words, the informal information base of an education-ist is a potential source of descriptions and judgements about various aspects of the educational world. The contents of the information base are not inert but can be reworked creatively by the owner to generate new understandings. This capacity to produce new understandings is further enhanced if informal information bases, rather than remaining isolated within individuals, are put in contact with those of others so that the collective contents are shared and collaboratively explored. The informal information bases of individuals constitute a potential information system. The existence of such a system within a coherent group of educationists is a *sine qua non* for any claim to collective professional knowledge and judgement. A personal information system is not a static entity. Flows of information occur all the time between the informal information bases both of colleagues within the professional group and those outside it. For example, the good adviser or inspector is in regular contact with the practice of teachers and thus the ideas which lie behind it. Furthermore, the informal information system will be in an interactive relationship with the formal information system.

The reader may wonder, 'Why all the talk about informal information bases and systems to describe the familiar experience that individuals have thoughts and ideas and sometimes share them?' There are several reasons. The current emphasis on information tends to be on the establishment of formal external systems. This is, of course, important. However, we should not forget that the information contained in such systems derives ultimately from individuals. Moreover, even if formal information systems are greatly improved from their present unsatisfactory state, the information held inside people's heads will continue to be influential in real-life decision making. How individuals use this information remains largely obscure. In addition, attempts to use the range of information individually held within the heads of a group are seldom systematic. Conventional ways of seeking to exploit the expertise and talents within a group, through team and committee meetings, are generally inadequate to the task, not least because of the personal dynamics that may prevail and the games which people habitually play in such settings.

The purpose of this section of the chapter is to suggest some structured approaches which may be used to access systematically the information held by individuals in order to construct new understandings of greater generality and inclusivity. Specifically two approaches will be outlined: the nominal group technique; the hermeneutic dialectic process.

145

The nominal group technique (NGT)

This is used in situations where individual judgements must be tapped and combined. It is described in detail in Delbecq *et al.* (1975). It involves a structured meeting of up to ten people. The meeting is focused on a specific issue or question. It is important that this is defined in precise terms. The conduct of the meeting is controlled by a leader and consists of six distinct steps.

1 *Silent generation of ideas in writing.* The question is presented to the group with some indication of the kind of information required. Group members are asked to write down their ideas on a sheet of paper, independently and without discussion. Interaction is discouraged to avoid dominance by individuals of the process of idea generation. It is important that the leader avoids providing answers to the question for the group.

2 *Round-robin recording of ideas.* The ideas generated are then shared within the group. This is done by the leader asking each member in turn to present an idea in a terse phrase, recorded on a flipchart. This procedure is repeated in further rounds until no new ideas are forthcoming. Ideas are presented without discussion and, wherever possible, in their original form. Members may pass when they have no item to present but may re-enter if an idea occurs to them subsequently. The procedure has the advantage of equalising the opportunity to present ideas.

3 *Serial discussion for clarification.* Members now decide whether any idea is merely a duplicate of one already given.The ideas listed on the flipchart are taken in order and a brief period is allowed for discussion of each. This enables members to ask questions, seek clarification and indicate agreement or disagreement with any item on the list. All items are given equal consideration. Clarification of any item can be attempted by any member. The purpose is to aid understanding and minimise any influence based on the talkativeness or status of individual members.

4 *Preliminary vote on item importance.* Each member is asked to select a specified number of priority items from the list. Each priority item is recorded on a card or rating form. The priority

items are then rank-ordered or rated. The leader collects the cards or rating forms, shuffles them to ensure anonymity and records the results on the flipchart.

5 *Discussion of the preliminary vote.* Voting patterns are examined and considered. The aim is to improve judgemental accuracy not to exert social pressure.

6 *Final vote.* This is a repeat of step 4 allowing accurate aggregation of group judgements and bringing the meeting to an end.

The technique is derived from social, psychological and management science studies of group processes.

An obvious application of the technique to our concerns here is to the formulation of evaluation priorities. This is the starting point for establishing a system-wide evaluation strategy. In the case of an LEA, the group might consist of a number of officers and inspectors, together with the chair of the education committee. The meeting gets under way by first considering the LEA's strategic plan for the next financial year. The appropriate NGT issue on which the team then works might be something along the following lines: 'Given the strategic plan, identify those aspects which, in your view, should be priorities for evaluation. Try to translate each of these into one or more broad questions which you would expect an evaluation to illuminate.' The leader of the group then lists the responses on a flipchart. This might be done using two columns (one for the aspects of the plan to be evaluated, the other giving the associated issues). Steps 2–6 of the NGT, as set out above, then follow. The end product is an agreed set of evaluation priorities with some indication of the issues to be considered.

The technique can also be adapted to be used as the principal vehicle for an evaluation. This would be most appropriate where there are several people knowledgeable about a particular evaluand and where a considered judgement on it needs to be delivered swiftly. As an example consider a school which has recently introduced a new system of pastoral care and for which an interim review is required for the headteacher. An NGT team is recruited consisting of the senior pastoral care staff and a representative sample of form tutors. The NGT leader is a member of staff with a detached perspective on the development. To achieve success in the NGT exercise the leader needs to be respected by participants and have the appropriate range of skills. The NGT question posed in this case might be: 'What detailed evidence do we have of the impact, beneficial or otherwise, made by the new pastoral care structure on pupil behaviour, staff relationships with pupils, school–parent relationships and the administrative responsibilities of staff?' The leader structures the recording of the group's ideas under two headings: nature of the impact; and examples of supporting evidence. Voting is conducted on the basis of the perceived importance of each agreed impact example. The outcome of the exercise provides the basis for a short report prepared by the group leader.

In the above example, complementary NGT sessions could be held with a sample of pupils. Indeed the use of the technique with pupil groups has been attempted by Froggatt (1988). He used the NGT as part of an evaluation study of an Individual Studies programme designed for Year 10 and 11 pupils.

The NGT has considerable potential as a key method in the evaluation repertoire of an inspectorate team. In particular it provides a very economical way of dealing with urgent requests for information on major developments which are not included as topics in the evaluation programme. Individual inspectors with some knowledge of the development concerned could be mobilised swiftly to act as an NGT group. Because an inspectorate team has a continuing existence, the opportunities of exploiting the NGT on a regular basis are considerable. A team can become highly skilled in the use of the technique. The NGT therefore acts as a powerful vehicle for developing coherent inspectorate judgements.

The hermeneutic dialectic process (HDP)

This is a term coined by Guba and Lincoln (1989) to denote a key feature in the latest formulation of their approach to evaluation. This somewhat impressive, and perhaps initially forbidding, term is to be understood in the following way:

> a hermeneutic/dialectic process . . . takes full advantage, and account of, the observer/observed interaction to create a constructed reality that is as informed and sophis- ticated as it can be made at a particular point in time.

The process is *hermeneutic* in that it is aimed toward developing improved (joint) constructions, a meaning closely associated with the more traditional use of the term to denote the process of evolving successively more sophisticated interpretations of historical or sacred writings. It is dialectic in that it involves the juxtaposition of conflicting ideas, forcing reconsideration of previous positions.

(Guba and Lincoln, 1989: 44; 89–90)

The starting point for using the process is to identify a key stakeholder group for a particular evaluand. The evaluator then selects an initial respondent from the group. The following stages then follow:

1 The evaluator engages the respondent (R_1) in an open-ended interview about his/her views on the evaluand. The aim is to elicit observations about claims, concerns and issues about the evaluand. R_1 is then asked to nominate another respondent, R_2, who is thought to hold very different views on the evaluand.

2 The claims, concerns and issues identified by R_1 are analysed to give a formulation of R_1's construction, designated C_1. This is done, ideally, for R_1 before R_2 is approached.

3 R_2 is then interviewed and his/her claims, concerns and issues elicited. When that is completed, R_2 is presented with the construction (C_1) derived from the previous respondent and is invited to comment. Not only, therefore, is information obtained from R_2 but also a critique on R_1's input and construction.

4 R_2 is asked for a nomination, R_3. The evaluator completes a second analysis to give a new construction, C_2, based on the two respondents R_1 and R_2.

5 R_3 is interviewed and then allowed to comment on C_2, and so on.

6 The process continues with further respondents, resulting in the formulation of ever more informed and sophisticated constructions. Initially the concern is to identify respondents who can enlarge the scope of the emerging constructions. Later the aim is to maximise the range of information collected. The process is terminated either when informational redundancy sets in or when two or more constructions fail to be reconciled.

7 When a hermeneutic circle is completed, it may be repeated a second time to give earlier respondents the chance to comment on the later constructions. It might also be repeated with another set of respondents similar to the first.
8 The cycle can be enriched by introducing constructions obtained from: other stakeholder groups; relevant documentation; observational data; the evaluator. No set of constructions, however, should be regarded as authoritative and therefore free from being challenged.

The process outlined above (1–8) is one of iterative interviews and construction formulation and may be regarded as an evaluation approach in its own right. Where stakeholder groups are few and small in number, as may be the case in reviewing the performance of a subject department in a school or college, the process may be carried out and completed within a day or so.

An approximation to the process might be said to take place in some TSAS inspections of YT schemes. Certainly the serial interviewing of trainees is a key feature of the TSAS inspection approach, and opportunities arise in later interviews to get trainees' views on comments expressed by those earlier in the interviewing cycle.

For Lincoln and Guba, however, the hermeneutic dialectic process is but a stage, albeit a key stage, in the total flow of activity associated with the conduct of an evaluation. Typically at the end of the cycle, some claims, concerns or issues remain unresolved by the consensual process. Some of these may represent the irreconcilable consequences of different value positions held by contending stakeholders. Others, however, may require the collection of information which, when added to existing constructions, may lead to reconstruction and thus the resolution of apparent differences. In those situations information may need to be collected through observations made during site visits, questionnaire surveys and perhaps further hermeneutic circles with other stakeholders.

Merits of the two methods

The NGT may be advantageous for the evaluation of programmes and policies of intermediate complexity where:

- the exercise needs to be completed within a single meeting;
- a small number of knowledgeable stakeholders and/or local experts can be identified;
- some interaction between members is desirable.

The HDP is used to advantage for evaluations of less complex, more discrete programmes where:

- the detailed views of a relatively small number of stakeholders are required;
- the aim is to develop more sophisticated and consensual understandings of the issues involved and to pinpoint areas where further investigation is necessary.

8

DATA COLLECTION AND ANALYSIS: 2

INTRODUCTION

The previous chapter outlined two of the three main sources of data on which the time-constrained evaluator may draw: existing documentation, and the personal information system. The purpose of this chapter is to deal with the third source: *condensed fieldwork*. All three methods, as I have already commented, are not rigidly discrete. In fact, condensed fieldwork will often use documents and records as an additional information source. Furthermore, the informal information system is a pervasive influence in condensed fieldwork as in all methods of enquiry. However, the distinction between the methods is worth preserving. Condensed fieldwork, although it may use existing information sources, is primarily concerned with the collection of new information, which is obtained by going out into the field and studying the evaluand *in situ*.

The fieldwork tradition has generally not been economical of time. For example, anthropologists have often spent long periods, amounting in some cases to several years, in the cultures which they seek to understand. Educational researchers studying the life of schools have usually carried out their investigations through regular visits conducted over periods of one or more years. One justification for lengthy periods of fieldwork is that organisations and cultures are complex. If they are to be understood by outsiders, time will be needed for the acquisition of an insider perspective: to gain access, secure trust and become familiar with the ways of thinking, the customs, the procedures and practices, and many other aspects of the everyday life of the insider. To conduct studies based on short periods in the field, so the argument goes, is to risk gaining a partial understanding, or even a distorted view, of the culture being investigated.

However, short periods of fieldwork can be said to characterise the institutional inspection approach of HMI. The same is true of the YT inspections of the TSAS. LEA inspectorates too are increasingly adopting similar styles of inspection, based on an apparently universal time quantum of five days at most per institution. How can such dramatically telescoped periods of fieldwork be justified?

First, they are justified by necessity. Monitoring and evaluation are central to the task of management at all levels. Consequently the range of possibilities for evaluation are legion. The reality is that these will always exceed the resources which can be realistically provided. It is not only a question of providing adequate resources for major innovations, although this may be difficult enough, as the experience of TVEI shows. There is also the need to evaluate the mainstream programmes and day-to-day activities which constitute the principal concerns of most organisations. There is absolutely no way in which the many individual components of a comprehensive monitoring and evaluation strategy, incorporating existing as well as innovative activities, can all be resourced on the scale of the research-style evaluations typically reported in the literature.

Second, if evaluation is to be of value then it needs to furnish useful information. Information which is specifically targetted towards user requirements and appears quickly and promptly is to be preferred to that which is of general interest and produced only after a substantial period of time. The production of information by condensed fieldwork is the only proposition which is feasible if evaluation is to be a regular and integral part of rational decision making and action.

Third, condensed fieldwork, at least as implicitly practised in inspection, does not involve encounters with totally novel environments and cultures as is the case in the anthropological tradition. Inspectors have, after all, been practitioners themselves and have had first-hand experience of teaching and educational management at a variety of levels. Therefore, although individual institutions and programmes will have many different characteristics, they are extremely unlikely to be completely unfamiliar to an inspector. Even on a first visit to a particular school or college, there will be many familiar features at hand which will enable inspectors to get an initial purchase on the institution and thus set their enquiries in train.

This initial familiarity with the objects of their inspection is expanded in two principal ways. An inspection is generally preceded by a study of documentation relevant to the institution or programme concerned. This enables inspectors to extend their general understanding of a particular class of evaluand by considering some aspects specific to the individual case. This will result, as previously mentioned, in a preliminary model of the evaluand. Furthermore, inspectors are likely to be involved with other examples of the evaluand on a regular basis. If these activities are carried out in a systematic and disciplined fashion, then inspectors will develop sophisticated and continually evolving schemata and typologies of schools. These will help inspectors to come to terms quickly with an individual school and thus carry through an effective evaluation with an economy of time.

Condensed fieldwork is justified on the grounds of necessity, utility and familiarity of the evaluator with the evaluand through training, experience and repeated practice. Condensed fieldwork which involves a team of evaluators, as in HMI-style institutional inspections, has two further justifications. First, although the duration of an institutional inspection is short, the total amount of inspector time may be considerable. For example, a full inspection of a large secondary school may involve up to twenty or so inspectors, the equivalent of a full-time evaluator working within the school for half the academic year. A further justification for team-based condensed fieldwork is that it brings to bear on a particular evaluand the multiple perspectives of many evaluators. These perspectives may be shared within the team and thus lead to a fuller understanding of the evaluand than would be achieved by a lone evaluator. One possible limitation is that it is difficult for condensed fieldwork to capture more than a snapshot in time and thus obtain a record of what is typical for the institution. Where fieldwork takes place over a longer period it is easier to get a sense of what characteristics and features of an institution are reasonably stable and to assess the pattern over the year.

Condensed fieldwork has been described in terms of a possible approach to external evaluation. Condensed fieldwork can also be carried out on an individual site by insiders rather than outsiders. This corresponds to what is usually described as self-evaluation. Most self-evaluations are unlikely to be conducted under conditions in which time and resources are not severely limited. Moreover, if self-evaluations are to be increasingly related to development planning, as suggested in chapter 3, they will need to be highly focused, be carried through swiftly, and have their results reported promptly. The methods used in condensed fieldwork are therefore likely to be much the same whether carried out by inspectors, other external evaluators or those within an institution or programme. A major aim of this chapter is to outline some techniques which might be used in condensed fieldwork by those who will be involved in time-constrained evaluation on a regular and continuing basis as well as by those for whom it will be a more occasional activity and one focused largely on their own institution or programme.

CONDENSED FIELDWORK: SINGLE EVALUATOR

For illustrative purposes I shall consider the evaluation of a mathematics department in a secondary school. Whether carried out as an inspection, an external evaluation or a self-evaluation, the methods employed will be essentially the same.

As we saw in chapter 6, the starting point of any evaluation is the formulation of one or more questions which identify the types of information which key stakeholders require in order to carry out important actions relating to the evaluand. Some examples of relevant information requirements are set out below.

Information required	Possible action
Are National Curriculum attainment targets covered by current schemes of work?	Revise schemes as necessary.
Are aspects of mathematics (attainments and attitudes) differentiated by gender?	Develop teaching strategies to minimise differentiation.

What assumptions are made concerning the basic number skills of pupils entering the school? Are these consolidated and further developed in the first year mathematics course?	Establish joint working party with teachers from feeder schools to review respective courses.
What is the range of pupil attainments in mathematics?	Report to governors and LEA, inform parents.
Are the learning tasks sufficiently challenging for pupils of all abilities?	Report to school's working party on *Realising pupils' potential.*
To what extent are the aims of the department (and relevant aims of the school) being achieved?	Contribute to school self-evaluation exercise.

As can be seen, evaluation issues and related information needs may be general or specific. The important point is that there should be clarity both about the type of information required from an evaluation and the ways in which it is intended that the information should be used. These matters should be decided before the evaluation begins. This will ensure that the enquiry has a general focus and that the evaluator is able to use the limited time available to the best advantage.

Methods of data collection

I shall consider here the two principal methods of data collection: observation and interviews. These, together with those described in the previous chapter, are methods which can be used for more extensive fieldwork studies as well as for other approaches to educational enquiry. Which methods are used in any particular case will depend on the nature and scope of the information requirements.

The use of the methods referred to above in condensed fieldwork will normally require some modification and relaxation of what are conventionally regarded as appropriate standards of research rigour. The purpose here will be to describe these modified versions rather than attempting an exhaustive treatment of each method as it is usually encountered in non-condensed fieldwork.

Observation

In much of conventional field research, observation has come to mean *participant observation*. Participant observation is where the observer acts as a genuine member of a particular group, and has a commitment to its outcomes, while at the same time being an observer of its activities and milieu. *Non-participant observation* is where the observer seeks to play the role of the non-involved observer. In classroom observation, the place on the spectrum may in part be decided in prior discussion with the teacher involved. It is also influenced by the nature of the lesson and the age group of pupils. Thus in observing a group work lesson the observer, moving from group to group, inevitably gets caught up in what is happening.

Observational methods may also be distinguished according to their position on a *structured–unstructured* continuum. At the structured end, methods entail using *a priori* categories tied to specific observable behaviours which are recorded on a regular timed basis. The prototype is the Flanders Interaction Analysis Categories (Flanders, 1970) which code different categories of teacher and pupil talk. At the unstructured end of the continuum are methods which look at behaviour holistically and beyond the strictly observable, to consider such aspects as the motives and intentions of the actors. Predetermined categories are not employed; meaning emerges from a progressive focusing of observation and from a subsequent detailed study of the data collected.

Highly structured observational schedules are unlikely to be useful in condensed fieldwork. They tend to focus on a narrow band of behaviours, not necessarily those of greatest educational interest. They lack the comprehensiveness of cover required to deal with the variety of contexts which a study of any educational institution or programme inevitably encounters. Equally the use of lightly unstructured methods will not be satisfactory. It is necessary to have some preliminary framework to focus one's observations, if only because it is impossible to observe and record everything.

In practice, the approach to observation will be somewhere between the two extremes. Observation needs to be guided by some sense of purpose, and therefore to use at least a preliminary framework, while at the same time allowing flexibility to respond to the dynamics of specific contexts. Most inspectorates appear to use lightly structured observational approaches. HMI, for example, have employed over the years a variety of *aide-mémoires* and schedules for specific and general inspection exercises. These have been designed to help focus the attention of inspection teams on pertinent features and to provide a structure for retrieval and writing.

Although such schedules vary in content according to the different aspects with which they are concerned, they tend to have a common general structure. This general structure is also apparent in the observational schedules being developed by LEA inspectorates. In essence, most schedules consist of an organising structure of headings representing what are considered to be the main features or dimensions of the aspect being evaluated. The headings are typically elaborated by a small number of prompts, questions or items. The collection of headings and additional details constitutes the general criteria, usually implicit rather than explicit, which are presumed to underlie the resulting judgements made by inspectors. Figure 8.1 shows a typical example of an observational schedule.

The criteria outlined in Figure 8.1 will not be met in every lesson of mathematics observed but provide a reminder of what may be looked for over a series of lessons. It will therefore usually be necessary for the evaluator to record observations in the form of *field notes*. These provide the raw material from which are ultimately derived the descriptive and evaluative comments of the final report.

Field notes

The writing of good field notes is essential to the conduct of successful condensed fieldwork. The task is not easy since, in order to use the limited period available for evaluation to the maximum, it is necessary to move from lesson to lesson and activity to activity with little free time in between. It is therefore

PROVISION

Do teaching strategies and methods maximise pupils' learning in relation to the target outcomes? In particular:

<u>Planning</u>
Does the scheme of work
- satisfy key stage requirements?
- include process skills as well as content?
- set firm, understood targets
  for pupils?
- allow for continuity and
  progression?
- avoid gender stereotyping?

Do the arrangements for monitoring and assessment:
- allow the pupils to demonstrate achievement and understanding?
- provide a coherent, systematic, continuous picture of pupil achievement?

<u>Delivery</u>
Is there evidence of:
- mathematics across the curriculum?
- investigative work?
- practical work?
- problem solving?
- mental/aural/oral work?
- individual/group/class work?

Is appropriate use made of:
- apparatus, calculators, computers?
- the environment?

Is mathematics teaching supported by:
- teachers of suitable experience and expertise?
- an appropriate school and /or departmental organisation?
- adequate accommodation and equipment?

OUTCOMES

Does pupil performance match intended targets in relation to their ability? In particular:

<u>Pupil achievements</u>
Do the learning experiences of the pupils
- develop mathematical skills?
- develop positive attitude to mathematics?
- allow them to comment constructively about their work?
- allow for an appropriate experience of the National Curriculum?

<u>Materials</u>
Is there evidence of
- display of pupils' work?
- other relevant display material?
- selection of material resources?

Figure 8.1 Example of an LEA's inspection criteria for mathematics

essential that notes are written on the spot. It is recognised that an evaluator making copious notes during lessons and other activities can sometimes be a somewhat intimidating presence. Note-taking should be done as discreetly as possible. Notes need to be brief and written up in fuller detail as soon as possible. This will often mean, in practice, using available lunch and tea breaks and periods at the end of the day to complete the task. The creation of detailed field notes is an inescapable requirement if good condensed fieldwork is to be accomplished.

The novitiate fieldworker often asks, 'What shall I observe?' and 'What shall I note down?' There seems to be so much going on in a classroom that it is difficult to know what to choose to record. This is why it is essential to establish clearly, before observation and data collection get under way, the purpose of the evaluation and therefore the kind of information being sought. Such information and the use of any schedule of the kind shown in Figure 8.1 will together provide a focus for observation, and therefore an indication of what to record. For example, in observing a mathematics lesson, notes on the methods of teaching, the learning task and the response of the pupils are likely to constitute a major part of any subsequent field note. The aim is to capture a slice of classroom life relevant to the concerns of the evaluation. In observations of situations in which events and activities unfold, as in classrooms or meetings, it is generally helpful for subsequent recall and regeneration of details to record things in chronological order.

The act of writing up field notes is also invaluable in forcing the fieldworker to think through the events of the day and to confront actively the data collected. The fieldworker is sensitised early on to possible themes, trends, inter-relationships and connections between various data elements. Writing field notes and thinking about their content constitute an essential preliminary to the processes of analysis and interpretation. These processes must begin during the fieldwork phase and not be left until the end of data collection when there will be too little time available to tackle an undigested mass of field notes. This issue of analysis is considered in more detail later.

Despite the crucial role played by field notes in qualitative and case study research and evaluation, there is a surprising dearth of practical advice about how to construct them (Burgess, 1982). The tendency seems to have been to assume that field notes are very much a reflection of the personality of the investigator and that general guidance on how they should be developed is inappropriate. Bogdan and Biklen (1982), however, provide some down-to-earth advice.

Since field notes will be continually referred to in the process of analysis, it is essential that they are clearly numbered and contain such basic details as: title; date when the observation was carried out; if different from the latter, the date when the field note was written; where the observation took place; who carried it out.

Most of the content of a field note will be a verbal description of the setting and activities observed. However, sketches and diagrams of the context in which observation takes place, for example classroom layout, may be usefully appended. In addition, it is useful to include more *reflective* sections in which the observer offers personal comment on the progress of the evaluation. Bogdan and Biklen suggest that reflective comments might deal with issues of:

- *analysis:* speculations about emerging themes and patterns, connections between pieces of data;
- *method:* details of procedures and strategies employed, rapport with subjects;
- *ethical dilemmas and conflicts;*
- *frame of mind:* awareness by the observer; preconceptions and assumptions about the setting being studied;
- *points of clarification*: earlier problems that have been resolved as the enquiry has progressed.

Where such comments are incorporated into the field notes they should be clearly demarcated from the main descriptive sections. In some cases extended reflective comments are better written up separately as memos.

It is useful to structure the organisation of field notes with generous use of margins, paragraphs and internal headings. This will help the subsequent process of analysis. As part of the latter it is often necessary to reorder the sequence of field notes so that related aspects can be conveniently brought together and scrutinised. Field notes are therefore best written up on one side of paper only with the separate sheets stored in a ring binder to allow easy detachment of individual examples.

The task of writing structured field notes from initial recordings made on the spot is not easy. However, as in other areas, frequent practice is an essential requirement for the successful development of the skills involved. The example of HM inspectors is instructive. They are constantly involved in writing up accounts of the many visits made to educational institutions and programmes, whether or not these are part of formal inspections. HM inspectors have for long been the only group of educationists who regularly record, throughout their working life, their observations of educational experience and provision. It is that feature of practice, perhaps more than any other, which accounts for the distinctive authority and credibility of HMI judgements. More recently, a comparable claim can be made in the training field through the emergence of the TSAS and its programme of regular inspections of YT schemes. LEA inspectorates too, as they develop systematic programmes of evaluation, will need to develop appropriate approaches to field note construction. The field notebook is the essential recording device of the inspector, or of anyone who engages in condensed fieldwork. It is from the contents of the field notebook that considered and expanded field notes are derived. It is the field notes which are the primary data sources from which the subsequent evaluation report is compiled.

The kind of notes envisaged for condensed fieldwork will generally be shorter than those which are often produced in more conventional approaches. This arises as a consequence of the more limited time available, the need to conduct a speedy analysis of the content of field notes and the fact that a focus for observation is usually apparent from the beginning. Field notes are usually seen only by those who compile them so that handwritten versions are quite acceptable. However, word-processed versions will always be easier to use in the analysis stage.

Other targets for observation

A special case of the use of observation in evaluation is the *chronolog* (Guba and Lincoln, 1981: 204). This often takes the form of a single day in the life of a subject. The chronolog is being increasingly used in inspections, where it frequently takes the form of shadowing a particular pupil throughout the school day. It can be regarded as one way of generating a sample of lessons to observe, seen from the perspective of an individual pupil.

In the evaluation of education and training programmes, the primary targets for observation include the activities of teachers and pupils, trainers and trainees, as they occur in a variety of learning environments and encounters. Looking at what happens in an individual classroom, for example, captures something of the complex, continuous and seamless web which constitutes pupil learning. The observer may be able to discern the immediate effects on the learning of pupils or trainees of a lesson or training session. What may not be apparent, however, is the cumulative effect of previous, unobserved lessons or activities. If an assessment of these is not made, an evaluation is likely to be little more than an assessment of decontextualised and isolated incidents.

An important area of observation is the work produced by pupils or trainees. Looking through notebooks will help to identify the sequence of learning which leads up to the lesson being observed. It will also indicate something of the nature of the learning demands being made on the pupil and the expectations of the teacher. Scrutiny of notebooks also gives an indication of the teaching methods adopted. For example, it is easy to discern where pupils have received a predominant diet of dictated or chalkboard notes. The capabilities of pupils may also be revealed by examining, where this is possible, the more extended and individual exercises represented by homework assignments and project work.

How, then, would the evaluator of a mathematics department go about tackling this aspect of observational enquiry? S/he will request, in advance of the evaluation visits, a sample of pupils' work drawn from each year group. This sample need not be large, possibly no more than the work of three pupils from each year group, covering a wide ability range, balanced by gender and, where appropriate, by ethnic origin. The task, which must be accomplished in at most a couple of hours, is to discover evidence of:

- the levels of attainment expected of, and reached by, pupils;
- the nature and appropriateness of the sequence of learning adopted;
- the range of teaching and learning methods used;
- the quality and regularity of teacher assessment of pupils' work.

A summary of the conclusions drawn from the exercise is made as a special field note. An alternative or additional approach is to spend some time during classroom observation looking at the notebooks of one or more pupils. In this case any comments would be included in the main field note for the session.

How well pupils learn is influenced by how well teachers teach. Both are influenced in turn by two important factors which require assessment. First, there is the question of the range and quality of the learning resources available to pupils. Effective teaching and learning require access to the appropriate resources at the right time. The evaluator looks not only at the mathematics textbooks used in the classes visited but also at the range of books, other materials, equipment and learning aids available within the department and/or the school. Evidence on such matters as accessibility and frequency of use is gleaned by direct observation made during a series of lesson visits. Additional information will be sought through discussion with teachers and perhaps through indirect questions to pupils.

The second factor is concerned with the nature of the support given to the individual teacher through the management structure. How well or badly lessons proceed in particular classrooms is in part influenced by how well the head of mathematics manages the department. For example, subject to the limitations of the budget – itself of course influenced by the decisions of the school's senior management – teachers may reasonably expect the head of the department to operate a rational system for ordering materials and equipment and straightforward procedures for ensuring that teachers and pupils have access to the range of learning resources available. Teachers should also expect professional support from the head of department and the headteacher. This will be manifested in the style of management adopted and in the ways individual issues and concerns are dealt with and resolved. The practice of management, unlike that of teaching, is difficult to identify in a way that can be directly observed. In most cases the quality of management support will be assessed indirectly. Possible methods include scrutiny of departmental and/or school documentation, attendance at staff meetings and assessing how management and administrative procedures impact on the staff. More detailed information on the quality and effects of management can also be obtained by interview or questionnaire survey of staff. This will require the prior knowledge and agreement of the managers concerned.

Multiple observational targets and field notes

It must already be apparent that a highly structured approach to observation would not be realistic. Even if specifically designed schedules were readily available, the time required for training in their use, applying them in a specific situation and analysing the results obtained would be difficult, if not impossible, to find under condensed fieldwork conditions. Moreover, such a collection of schedules would be unlikely to be responsive to the changing dynamics of organisations as intricate as school departments. Condensed fieldwork requires the kind of flexibility which only the human instrument is able to provide. The strength of a lightly structured and focused approach lies not in the use of tightly defined *a priori* categories of conventional observational approaches but, as we will see later, in the methods of inductive analysis which are subsequently applied to the field note data.

Interviewing

Approaches to interviewing can also be located on a structured–unstructured continuum. At the structured end, reliance is placed on the use of a carefully constructed interview schedule made up of a number of precisely focused and worded questions. Structured interviews resemble orally administered questionnaires. A tightly structured interview schedule tends to be used where the interviewer has a fairly clear model, theory or view of the entity being investigated.

At the other end of the continuum are interviews which are open-ended and which allow interviewees to talk freely about the topic under consideration. The content of the interview is very much more under the control of the interviewee. The interviewer will also generally have a less definite conceptualisation of the topic or theme, and will want to encourage interviewees to reveal the details and depths of their personal views and opinions.

In practice, as with observation, an intermediate approach is frequently employed in fieldwork and case study research. That is to say, the interviewer will have a number of general issues and concerns to explore but will be relatively relaxed about the manner and order of their elicitation. Interviewees will be encouraged to talk about their views on the particular theme of the interview. In so doing, some of the interviewer's specific questions may be addressed naturally; if not, the interviewee's responses will be sought directly. In other words, the loose structure of issues constitutes a series of prompts which the interviewer intersperses, where appropriate, in the interviewee's flow of talk.

Good interviews are those where interviewees talk freely and to the point about their views, opinions and feelings. Under these conditions, even a short interview may generate a rich store of perspectives. In normal fieldwork it is common practice to record interviews. The recordings can then be played back and studied at leisure. Often typed transcripts of the interviews are prepared so that they can be analysed in detail later. This is not a realistic proposition in condensed fieldwork.

The use of large samples of interviewees is usually precluded in condensed fieldwork. In some cases this may not be a problem since the population of relevant interviewees may be sufficiently small in number for all members to be involved. For instance, in our example of the evaluation of secondary school mathematics, it may well be feasible for the evaluator to interview the head of department and the subject teachers. For pupil interview, however, selection would be vital.

Another way of dealing with the issue of interview samples in condensed fieldwork is to use *group interviewing*. In this way the views of a larger number of subjects can be obtained. Group interviews bring together a number of people who are encouraged to talk about the topic of interest under the guidance and coordination of the interviewer. The method might be used with teachers, parents and even with pupils. Managing the personal dynamics of such groups, while at the same time keeping discussion on track, and encouraging everyone to contribute is a more complex task than individual interviewing. The interviewer will be fully stretched without having to assume the additional responsibility of keeping notes. It is sometimes possible to have the note-taking task undertaken by a colleague evaluator.

In practice, interviewing is not always a formal activity, separate from observation. Individual teachers may be interviewed more naturally and conveniently in the contexts in which they are observed. This may take place before or more often at the end of the lesson. In such informal situations the term interviewing is perhaps something of a misnomer. Purposeful conversations may be a description nearer the mark. Teacher views will therefore often be incorporated within the observational field note. Pupil views may also be sought naturally in context by going round the classroom looking at work being done and discreetly asking the occasional question. However, where formal or semi-formal interviews are undertaken it will be necessary to record the details in separate field notes. The latter, like those concerned with observation, will be written up from the briefer notes made on the spot.

Pupil interviewing, of whatever form, needs to be arranged in advance, and may be disruptive of pupils' timetables. A better approach is for the evaluator to negotiate with the teacher an arrangement for talking briefly to individual pupils while they are at work. Such occasions also provide an opportunity for the evaluator to question pupils on what they are learning and thus get some indication of any difficulties being experienced.

Sometimes it may be convenient to use a questionnaire. Questionnaires need to be easily and quickly completed. It is also essential that the results from questionnaires can be rapidly analysed so that they are available for use with minimal delay. This means that questionnaires should be brief and composed of items requiring short or closed responses.

There are two areas in particular where the teacher's view is vital. The first is where the evaluator observes an individual lesson. In order to make a sound assessment of a lesson an evaluator needs information which only the teacher concerned can provide: the purpose of the lesson; its location within the sequential development of lessons in the curriculum area concerned; and the teacher's assessment of how the lesson went. This information can often be obtained naturally in conversation with the teacher before and after the lesson. It is also important in discussion with teachers to identify those factors which are perceived as facilitating or inhibiting their educational aims. These are likely to throw some light on the quality of the management structures in the school and how they act to support the classroom teacher. Here too the use of short questionnaires may be an appropriate alternative to interviewing.

Evaluation design

The content of the decisions taken by an evaluator about how, when, where and with whom to carry out an evaluation constitute the design. The design of an evaluation based on condensed fieldwork, although initially structured, progressively evolves as the evaluation proceeds. The starting point for determining the design is to have a preliminary conceptual framework of the evaluand.

Figure 8.2 represents a department in line management to the headteacher and senior staff, and the areas of decision making which give rise to effective teaching. Variations on this model are, of course, possible, given different managerial or decision-making structures.

The framework provides a model which enables the evaluator to plan a preliminary design, including provisional choices about the sampling and evaluation methods to be used. An evaluator of a mathematics department will almost certainly want to sample teaching programmes and, in so doing, see all teachers and a sample of pupil groups representing the full range of ability. The nature of the sample will be determined by the scope of the evaluation and the time available. Sampling in condensed fieldwork is not governed by principles of randomness or representativeness. Condensed fieldwork uses *purposeful sampling*. Subjects are chosen for the purpose of providing information relevant to the specific concerns of the evaluation.

By considering the conceptual framework, the evaluator will be able to make provisional decisions about what to observe,

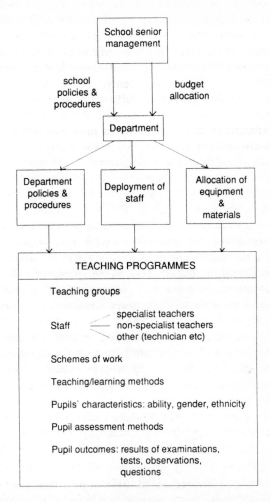

Figure 8.2 Model of a secondary school subject department

whom to interview, what sequence of activities to follow and
the likely amounts of time to be allocated to each. The evaluation
design for the first day should be prepared in some detail and
that for subsequent days much more tentatively, and in outline
form. A design, and therefore a clear indication of how to
proceed with an evaluation, is required from the outset if
the limited time available is to be used to the full. Yet the

design should not be regarded as sacrosanct. Its purpose is to get the evaluation under way effectively and swiftly, and to allow for continual modification as data are collected and considered. The evaluator must be prepared to change tack as a deeper understanding of the evaluand emerges in the course of interacting with it.

As we shall see in the next section, data are not simply collected and put on one side for later analysis and interpretation. All three processes go on simultaneously. As the evaluation proceeds, unexpected, interesting or disturbing things may come to light which need to be pursued. To do so will often require changes in the planned programme of evaluation activities: sessions may need to be observed, further people interviewed and fresh documents examined. As the data come in, the evaluator will be forming provisional ideas and judgements about the evaluand which will require testing. This will necessitate changes being made in the questions to be asked and in the aspects to be observed. The aim of the evaluation is to ground a developing understanding of the evaluand in data as they are collected. This requires an evaluator to modify any explanatory frameworks and models which do not fit the data. In other words, the conduct of condensed fieldwork is initiated in a semi-structured *deductive* mode through the use of a provisional framework or model but develops thereafter through an essentially *inductive* approach.

The analysis of data

At the end of a period of condensed fieldwork the evaluator will have a collection of field notes that may run to many pages. These will require analysis if they are to be of help in answering the questions posed at the outset of the evaluation. Condensed fieldwork shares a fundamental problem with other forms of qualitative research. In qualitative research, unlike quantitative, there are few agreed canons for the conduct of data analysis. As Miles and Huberman comment:

> We have the unappealing double blind whereby qualitative studies can't be verified because researchers don't report

170

on their methodology, and they don't report on their methodology because there are no established canons or conventions for doing so.

(Miles and Huberman, 1984: 244)

The situation is no better in qualitative evaluation. Furthermore, where qualitative evaluation is conducted under extreme conditions of time-constraint, employing condensed fieldwork, the absence of methodological guidance is even more complete. One of the purposes of this book is to draw attention to this significant *lacuna* in the repertoire of evaluation methodology and to indicate how the situation might be improved.

In a class on its own, however, is the systematic attempt made by Miles and Huberman (1984) to develop a detailed set of procedures for the analysis of data in qualitative research, having a rigour and an acceptability comparable to those which are employed in quantitative research. Although their approach is geared to the general field of qualitative case study research, I believe it to be adaptable to the special needs of evaluators operating under condensed fieldwork conditions. This section therefore draws on their approach.

Categories and codes

The starting point for analysis is the collection of field notes, including interview transcripts and relevant document summaries, which have accumulated throughout the evaluation. In their usual narrative form, field notes are difficult to analyse, particularly if they are lengthy and many. The first stage of data reduction is to divide the field notes into meaningful segments corresponding to one or more sentences of text. The segments define categories representing recurring themes, patterns and regularities which become apparent when the field notes are systematically read through. Each category is operationally defined, named and coded. Codes are essentially organising and retrieval devices.

Codes can be obtained in two principal ways. They may be derived inductively by scrutinising the data after they have been collected. Figure 8.3 is a section from the transcripts of a series of interviews carried out some years ago

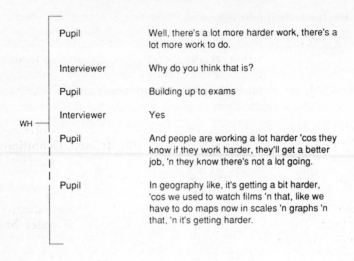

	Pupil	Well, there's a lot more harder work, there's a lot more work to do.
	Interviewer	Why do you think that is?
	Pupil	Building up to exams
WH	Interviewer	Yes
	Pupil	And people are working a lot harder 'cos they know if they work harder, they'll get a better job, 'n they know there's not a lot going.
	Pupil	In geography like, it's getting a bit harder, 'cos we used to watch films 'n that, like we have to do maps now in scales 'n graphs 'n that, 'n it's getting harder.

(code WH = work harder)

Figure 8.3 Example of a coded section of an interview transcript

on perceptions of school life of pupils in the fourth year of secondary school.

Alternatively, codes may be formulated in advance of fieldwork from a consideration of the conceptual framework, the list of research questions and the provisional hypotheses that the researcher brings to the study. This is the approach preferred by Miles and Huberman who recommend the creation of a start list of codes. In a major study of school improvement they successfully employed a start list of over ninety codes. They claim that this number of codes can be easily retained in the memory, without constant reference to the list, provided it is well structured. Their list had codes organised under nine general headings. For example, one of the headings was designated site dynamics and transformations. This grouped together thirteen separate codes. Two will give a flavour of the approach.

Initial user experience:

TR-START   Emotions, events, problems or concerns, assessments, made by teachers and administrators during the first six weeks of implementation.

172

Implementation problems:

TR-PROBS Difficulties or concerns relating to implementation at the personal, classroom, organisational, extra-organisational levels, including
reasons given for presence of difficulty or
concern.

As can be seen, each category is defined and given a title and
a code. Each category is relatively broadly defined. Definitions
which are too narrow and specific will result in excessively
lengthy and unwieldy lists, lacking organising power.

Under conditions of condensed fieldwork it is unlikely that
there will be sufficient time to develop codes by the inductive
method. The use of a predetermined start list of codes has
much to commend it, particularly where an evaluator frequently encounters the same class of evaluand. For a novel
or one-off evaluation, the inductive approach to coding may
be appropriate. If the evaluation involves condensed fieldwork,
it is more realistic to use a combination of these two main
approaches: a prior set of general codes within which more
content-specific codes would be developed inductively as the
data were collected.

The process of coding field notes cannot be left until the end
of data collection but should be carried out regularly during
the course of the evaluation. To the discipline of writing up
field notes at the end of each day is added the further task
of coding. Not every piece of text in the field notes will need
coding: only those that relate to the specific concerns of the
evaluation. Moreover, a particular sequence of field notes will
need to use only a few of the codes available. Coding then,
particularly with practice, may be carried out quite quickly.

As the process of coding field notes proceeds, the evaluator
may become increasingly aware of the emergence of more
general, overarching themes or constructs which pull together
several coded segments. This is the beginning of a process of
moving from description and classification to understanding
and explanation. Miles and Huberman refer to these more
inclusive units of analysis as *pattern codes*. These should be
regarded as tentative: they will survive, become modified or be
rejected as they are tried out on further batches of field notes
and checked out against rival explanations and the views of

key informants. Sometimes pattern codes may be sufficiently robust to emerge as final organising themes of an evaluation. Some years ago the author was concerned with the evaluation of social education programmes in secondary schools. When the codings of the collection of observational field notes were reviewed, it was apparent that the content of much of the teaching in social education could be understood in terms of how teachers responded to three fundamental dichotomous issues. These issues, which effectively acted as pattern codes in the analysis, were as follows: knowledge-based *versus* skills-based approaches; exposition *versus* experiential learning; and passive acceptance *versus* critical debate (Wilcox *et al.*, 1984: 93–107). Usually, however, pattern codes are a staging post on the way to final conclusions. Further data analysis beyond that of simply scanning the coded field notes is normally necessary.

It is tedious and time-consuming to search through lengthy or numerous field notes to locate particular segments of text, particularly as, in narrative text, it is difficult to discern underlying regularities, relationships and themes. Complex field note collections therefore require further organisation before they can be readily used for data analysis. Notes are photocopied and cut into coded sections on which the source page numbers have been recorded. Some may be coded for more than one category and a copy for each is therefore needed. The sections are then sorted ready for further analysis. Computer programs to handle field notes have recently been developed, providing greater flexibility in both storage and retrieval.

The inductive derivation of codes during or after data collection for the purpose of analysis is a different process from that which uses predetermined criteria as a means of guiding and structuring observation. However, if codes and categories are generated in advance of data collection, as Miles and Huberman suggest, the two processes become less distinct.

CONDENSED FIELDWORK: EVALUATION TEAMS

Condensed fieldwork as outlined so far has been described largely in terms of a lone evaluator working on a single site. Condensed fieldwork involving two or more evaluators may also be encountered in the form of: externally or locally funded evaluation teams; inspection teams; and groups of staff carrying out self-evaluation exercises. It is useful to distinguish between evaluation teams working on a single site and those involved on several.

Multiple evaluators on a single site

Undoubtedly the most developed example of condensed field-work involving multiple evaluators on a single site is the HMI model for institutional inspections. This model has profoundly influenced the more recent inspection activities of the TSAS and LEA inspectorates.

The inspection model relies on the principle of the division of labour. Inspectors concentrate on those particular aspects of the institution in which they are specialists and, as such, follow the processes for the single evaluator. In addition, inspectors are expected to provide written notes on cross-curricular themes and school-wide functions, in-service training and the management of the school. Each such area will be coordinated by lead inspectors who will integrate their own observations with those of colleagues. Specialist and lead inspectors have the responsibility for reducing and transforming a substantial body of data into the form of draft sections, often no more than a page or two in length, which the reporting inspector brings together as the draft inspection report.

If an inspection, or indeed any evaluation based on con-densed fieldwork, is to have credibility it is necessary to be able to show, if required: a collection of written-up field notes; the products of data reduction; and the various decision rules used in these processes. Such a collection of material is analogous to what, in the context of case-study research, Stenhouse (1982) referred to as the case record. He suggests that good organisation of the case record is crucial for writing up the case study. So, too, with the inspection record which constitutes a sound evidential base which may confidently be made accessible to external scrutiny.

Multiple evaluators on multiple sites

There are two main examples here. A single team of evaluators may work across several sites. Many of the multi-site evaluations in the literature are of this type. Often each evaluator in the team works exclusively on a site or sites. At other times evaluation teams work on separate sites. In both cases the results of these evaluations are aggregated. A major aim of both approaches is to develop cross-site comparisons and thus give rise to descriptions and judgements of greater generality than those which apply to individual sites.

Pulling together the results obtained from multi-site studies is a notoriously difficult task, not least because each site will yield a formidable mass of field notes and other material. Miles and Huberman (1984) suggest starting with a master chart or *meta-matrix* which assembles the descriptive data from each site. The task is made considerably easier if a standardised approach involving common codes and reporting formats has been agreed between the site evaluation teams.

The initial meta-matrix should be developed from a consideration of the main questions posed for the evaluation. The data relevant to these questions are then summarised in the corresponding cells of the matrix for each of the sites. These summaries are obtained by scrutinising the site reports, if available, and/or the original site matrices and reducing and abbreviating the narrative text into short quotations, phrases, ratings or symbols. Reference back to the written-up field notes should not be necessary. Figure 8.4 is an example of a possible meta-matrix which brings together data relevant to a project on the tenth and eleventh year curriculum involving three secondary schools. The columns represent responses to the four basic questions posed:

- What success did the project have?
- What aspects did not go as well as hoped?
- What were the effects on the school and staff generally?
- What lessons were learned from the project?

The rows correspond to three sets of staff in each school.

The meta-matrix is then used to generate other matrices which examine in more detail the relationships between specific features of the evaluand. There are two main techniques: *partitioning*, dividing the data in new ways, and *clustering*, combining aspects of the data which seem to go together in some way. For example, column 3 might be partitioned to distinguish beneficial effects from those considered harmful, and column 4 clustered to group the lessons learned under

School	Teachers	(1) Project successes	(2) Less successful aspects	(3) Effects on school and staff	(4) Lessons learned
A	Headteacher and senior staff				
	Project teachers				
	Other teachers				
B	Headteacher and senior staff	Improved staff understanding of pupils; better social development of pupils	Failure to improve pupil attendance; poor information flow between schools; insufficient preparation time	Opportunity for staff to examine purposes, methods etc. of curriculum development	Importance of releasing staff time to make changes possible
	Project teachers				
	Other teachers				
C	Headteacher and senior staff				
	Project teachers				
	Other teachers				

Figure 8.4 **Example of a meta-matrix showing effects of an innovative project with one row completed for illustration** *Source:* **Adapted from Wilcox *et al.* 1984: 193 – 223**

a smaller number of cross-site general categories. As analysis proceeds, matrices become more ordered, as sites are sorted from high to low on some important factor – for example, the degree of project implementation – and thus move from being essentially descriptive to more relational and explanatory. It is essential that a record be kept of the decision rules which are used at each stage in the construction of matrices and the treatment of data.

The analytic procedures developed by Miles and Huberman are based on their experience of qualitative research studies carried out on multiple sites over one or more years. How is it, then, that their approach is relevant to the time-constrained evaluator? Is it realistic to suppose that multi-site evaluations can be carried out under conditions of condensed fieldwork? Surely complex innovations taking place in many institutions, as in TVEI, require long-term evaluation if they are to yield useful and valid information? Indeed, most evaluations of TVEI were funded on that assumption.

It will be recalled that evaluations can be located on a continuum ranging from the near instantaneity of everyday judgement to the more sustained and protracted enquiries typically described in the conventional evaluation literature. The evaluations of some major developmental initiatives will undoubtedly justify an evaluation design which is not as severely limited as that of those conducted under conditions of time-constraint. Time-constrained evaluation is a response to two obdurate facts of life. The first is that there will never be sufficient time and other resources available to carry out lengthy investigations into the complete range of activities which constitute the day-to-day running of complex organisations. Time-constrained evaluation is an attempt to extend the coverage of evaluation within levels of resourcing which are realistic. The second fact is that lengthy evaluations, while they may have contributed to greater generalised understanding, have very often not been of demonstrable use to those involved with the evaluands concerned. A major problem has been the repeated failure to deliver information to users in a swift and timely fashion.

The allocation of temporal and other resources to individual evaluations is a decision which is inevitably influenced by issues of perceived importance and political salience. Major projects such as TVEI may well be cases where extended evaluations are judged desirable. Having said that, however, even a substantial evaluation may be carried out as a series of individual time-constrained exercises, each of which addresses specific information needs as they emerge over time.

An alternative approach to multi-site evaluations is illustrated by the practice of HMI. Towards the end of an institutional inspection it is usual, in addition to drafting the sections of what will become the inspection report, for the team of inspectors to complete a standard questionnaire. This effectively summarises the conclusions and judgements of the inspection in terms of ratings and short responses to a series of individual questions. The results of the completed questionnaire may later be combined with those from other inspections. While this may lack the comparative and contrastive analysis of the Miles and Huberman approach, it does allow descriptions to be made of a class of institutions beyond that of individual exemplars.

Further alternatives will be necessary when a multi-site report is required and where it has not been possible, for whatever reason, to develop prior individual site analyses. One possibility here would be to survey the institutions by means of a suitable questionnaire. Indeed the original study from which Figure 8.4 was derived was based on the use of short questionnaires completed by the teaching staff in the schools involved in the project.

CONCLUSION

Although the notion of condensed fieldwork is but briefly alluded to in the literature, it is in reality a major means of carrying out practical evaluations. In particular, the activities of national and local inspectorates are the best exemplars of condensed fieldwork, albeit largely unrecognised as such. What is lacking, however, is an explicit and widely agreed methodology to underpin the practice of condensed fieldwork. The purpose of this chapter has been to sketch out the basis for such a methodology. It has concentrated on the processes of data collection and analysis and has emphasised the crucial tasks of field-note construction and analysis. The chapter has sought to show how the procedures devised by Miles and Huberman, although not originally conceived as such, can provide a useful basis for data analysis in condensed fieldwork. Anyone involved in the practical exigencies of evaluation in LEAs, TECs, institutions and programmes inevitably has to be eclectic in the use of methods. It is essential, however, that the methods used, and the techniques of data analysis which follow from them, should be capable of explicit description and open to scrutiny. This chapter is a contribution to that end.

9

DEVELOPING TRUSTWORTHY CONCLUSIONS

The main concern of this chapter is the development of trustworthy conclusions from evaluation. This will be addressed in three ways. First, some procedures for assessing trustworthiness will be outlined. Second, some indication will be given of how completed evaluations may be externally audited. Third, the formulation of judgements will be considered as a special case of evaluation conclusions. In particular, the implicit model which underlies the notion of inspectorate judgement will be elaborated. Finally the chapter suggests ways in which the conclusions of evaluation may be reported.

ASSESSING TRUSTWORTHINESS

The principal task of the evaluator is to find meaning in the data which have been collected. Meaning emerges as the field note data are examined; becomes more refined as the process of coding gets under way; is continued further as the data are subjected to analysis. Meanings, as they progressively emerge, are eventually incorporated within descriptions, explanations and judgements about the evaluand. It is these which constitute the conclusions of an evaluation.

Why should someone encountering the conclusions of an evaluation, whether in the form of a report or an oral presentation, believe that they are true? Trustworthiness is an issue which all forms of qualitative enquiry and research must face. The problem is that it is not easy to apply the criteria for judging the rigour of conventional research to the conduct and outcomes of qualitative research. There are two reasons for this. First, the criteria are related to the use of quantitative measuring instruments and are defined in terms of statistical procedures. Second, the criteria are derived from positivist assumptions about the nature of reality which many qualitative researchers either reject or at least regard with some scepticism. In qualitative research there are, however, no widely agreed alternative criteria, although the situation is beginning to change (see Hopkins *et al.*, 1989).

One attempt to develop alternative criteria is that of Lincoln and Guba (Lincoln and Guba, 1985; Guba and Lincoln, 1989). The practical implications of these criteria are potentially helpful to all qualitative evaluators whether or not they identify fully with the strong anti-positivist stance on which the evaluation approach of Lincoln and Guba is avowedly based.

Credibility

Lincoln and Guba propose the criterion of *credibility* as the equivalent to that of *internal validity* in conventional research. Internal validity is concerned with the extent to which an enquiry establishes how things really are. The notion of credibility, however, reflects a scepticism about a presumed actual reality 'out there'. It recognises the necessity of establishing a framework of constructed realities which are derived from those originally associated with respondents and the evaluator. This does not consist of simply adding the constructions of the evaluator to those of the various respondents. The constructions should become increasingly shared as they are fed back to respondents. The outcome of an evaluation should then ideally consist of a set of constructions, more sophisticated and comprehensive than were those of any participant – including the evaluator – at the start of the evaluation, which become accepted as an adequate account of 'how things are'.

Lincoln and Guba suggest several techniques for enhancing credibility.

Prolonged engagement

Substantial involvement on the site will help the evaluator to understand the culture, establish trust and minimise the effects of misinformation, distortion and any tendencies for respondents to be uncommunicative to, or conspire against, the evaluator. The achievement of prolonged engagement is a logical impossibility for any one specific time-constrained evaluation. However, it can be said to occur where different examples of a general class of entity are regularly evaluated. This transfer effect of experience gained in previous evaluations may be the justification behind the following comment of Miles and Huberman:

> We reiterate that people who are discreet, savvy in the environment under study, and conceptually ecumenical are often able to get to the core of a site in a matter of days, sidestepping . . . researcher bias and coming away with higher quality data than others could have compiled after several months' work.
>
> (Miles and Huberman, 1984: 234)

Prolonged engagement would seem to be a characteristic of self-evaluations, since those involved will be familiar with their own institution or programme as perceptive members of staff, if not as regular evaluators. How far their individual constructions of reality can be shared and developed further will depend on the kind of climate of trust and collegiality which exists among the staff.

Persistent observation

This involves identifying the characteristics and elements which are most relevant to the evaluation, and concentrating on these in detail. It is only by observing at first hand the things that really count that evaluators can progressively test out their emerging understandings and constructions. The process will be facilitated by clearly specifying in advance, in the form of information requirements, the purposes of the evaluation. In other words, knowing what to look for is advantageous, particularly for time-constrained evaluations. However, a pitfall to avoid is to focus observations prematurely and thus miss essential aspects of the evaluand. To do so is to risk the formulation of partial, distorted or even inaccurate constructions.

Triangulation

This is perhaps the most commonly recommended procedure for increasing the credibility of qualitative enquiry. In brief it involves the collection of different kinds of data so that these can be subsequently used to corroborate one another. Triangulation may involve the use of multiple and different sources, methods and evaluators. The use of different sources may imply multiple instances of one type of source, information from different interviewees or different sources of the same information, comparing a description of an event given by an interviewee with that to be found in some document. The use of different methods may imply either different techniques of data collection or different evaluation designs. The use of different evaluators is a practical proposition in an evaluation team, particularly where, as in an inspection, assessments are required of complex, cross-institutional aspects which are not the specialist preserve of any one evaluator.

Peer debriefing

This involves an evaluator engaging with a disinterested peer in an extended discussion about all aspects of the evaluation as it progressively unfolds. The role of peers is to pose searching questions in order to help evaluators to understand better the evaluation and their role within it, and to assess critically the methods used and the quality of the emerging findings. Peer debriefing may be a feasible proposition in well resourced evaluations which take place over a substantial period of time. It is unlikely to be a realistic option for time-constrained evaluations. In team evaluations, however, some of the benefits of peer debriefing may accrue through the interactions, both formal and informal, that occur between evaluators on site.

Negative case analysis

This may be regarded as the process of revising emerging hypotheses with hindsight. In principle the object is continuously to revise a hypothesis until it accounts for all known cases without exception. In practice, insistence on zero exceptions may be too rigid and impossible to satisfy in actual evaluations. Given the variability in human situations, it is more realistic to expect a hypothesis to fit a reasonable number of cases rather than to accommodate them all. This leads then to the question: 'What is a reasonable number?' The answer will depend on the nature of the aspect which is the subject of the hypothesis. Some aspects are inherently more difficult to assess than others. The location of the cut-off point is ultimately a matter of judgement. The choice of what proportion of cases might reasonably be taken as exemplifying a hypothesis might be made in advance of an evaluation rather like the selection of statistical confidence levels in a conventional quantitative study.

Member checks

Member checks occur where the analytic categories, interpretations and conclusions of an evaluation are tested with members of the stakeholding groups from whom the data were collected. Lincoln and Guba regard this as the single most crucial technique for establishing credibility. Member checks can take place regularly throughout an evaluation and also at its end when a feedback session to respondents may be arranged and, again later still, when a draft report may be available. Checks can be formal or informal procedures involving individuals and groups. Member checks serve a number of purposes, namely to provide opportunities for respondents: to clarify intentions; to correct factual errors and challenge interpretations; to volunteer additional information; and to comment on the adequacy of the evaluation in part or whole.

Transferability

In the conventional paradigm the onus is upon the investigator to demonstrate to what extent the findings of research apply beyond the particular study involved. This is essentially the issue of *external validity* or *generalisability*. In a naturalistic enquiry the purpose is to establish working hypotheses which apply in a specific context and at a specific time. Whether or not such hypotheses apply to other places, or to the same place at a different time, will presumably depend on the degree of similarity between their contexts and that of the original enquiry. Lincoln and Guba propose the term *transferability* to describe situations in which working hypotheses do hold up elsewhere.

In naturalistic enquiry the burden of proof of transferability lies not with the investigator but with others who might encounter the results subsequently in the form of a report or case study:

> It is the reader who has to ask, what is there in this study that I can apply to my own situation, and what clearly does not apply?
>
> (Walker, 1980: 34)

This will depend on the extent to which the report provides appropriately rich description of context – so-called *thick description*. The reports of time-constrained evaluations, however, as I shall indicate later, are likely to be short and characterised by thin rather than thick description. The transferability of individual time-constrained evaluations will therefore be relatively limited. However, as implied previously, the formulation of hypotheses in the context of multiple-site evaluations can be examined with a view to seeking regularities and patterns in the data which may lead to the formulation of statements of wider applicability than those derived from the individual constituent evaluations.

Dependability and confirmability

Two other fundamental issues of conventional research are those of reliability and objectivity. *Reliability* is concerned with consistency in the production of results. It rests on the assumption that, in principle, every repetition of the same methods to the same phenomena should give the same results. The achievement of high reliability requires particularly the use of instruments with constant and known characteristics. *Objectivity* seeks to ensure that the findings of research are determined only by the subjects and conditions of the study and not by the biases or interests of the researcher. It is assumed that the effects of human bias or distortion will be reduced, if not eliminated, by the use of the experimental method.

Both of these concepts need some modification where the infinitely adaptive human being is the main instrument and the research design is emergent and naturalistic rather than predetermined and experimental. In such situations Lincoln and Guba propose the terms *dependability* and *confirmability*. They associate dependability with the process of an enquiry and the extent to which it is established, trackable and documented. Confirmability is concerned with the product of an enquiry and the assurance that the integrity of findings is properly rooted in the data.

The external audit

The major technique which Lincoln and Guba propose for establishing dependability and confirmability is the *external audit*. In setting out the procedures involved in an audit they draw on the pioneering work of Halpern (1983). In order to carry out an audit there must be a residue of records stemming from the enquiry: the *audit trail*. This consists of the following possible categories of data:

- *raw data*: sound and video recordings, raw field notes, documents and records, survey results;
- *data reduction and analysis products*: written-up field notes, summaries, theoretical notes including working hypotheses;
- *data reconstruction and synthesis products*: structures of categories, findings and conclusions, final report;
- *process notes*: methodological notes including procedures and designs, trustworthiness notes relating to credibility, dependability and confirmability;
- *materials relating to intentions and dispositions*: enquiry proposal, personal notes and expectations;
- *instrument development information*: schedules, observation formats and surveys.

This list of categories gives the full range of information that might be available. No single enquiry is likely to include them all.

The *dependability* of an enquiry may be evaluated by an auditor examining the audit trail using a systematic set of steps and procedures. This would involve separate assessments being made of:

- the appropriateness of enquiry decisions and methodological shifts;
- the degree and incidence of enquirer bias;
- the overall design and implementation of efforts, and integration of the outcomes for dependability.

Each of these assessments requires the auditor to carry out a number of specific tasks. For example, an assessment of enquirer bias involves:

- identifying decisions and rationale which define the enquiry;
- identifying premature judgements;
- assessing whether there are any Hawthorne effects;
- determining whether enquirer is biased through naïveté;
- determining appropriateness of sampling decisions;
- evaluating the rationale for design decisions.

An evaluation of *confirmability* likewise involves a number of individual assessments of:

- whether findings are grounded in data;
- whether inferences are logical;
- utility of category structure;
- degree of incidence of enquirer bias;
- accommodation strategies.

Again, each of these assessments is related to several specific tasks. Thus the last item in the list, accommodation strategies, requires specific assessments of the efforts made during the enquiry to ensure confirmability, the extent to which negative evidence was taken into account and the accommodation of negative examples.

Miles and Huberman (1984) have developed the notion of the audit trail further by encouraging the researcher to document the procedures used during the conduct of a study. They propose the use of a series of forms outlining the procedures used for sampling, development of instrumentation, data collection and data analysis. For example, the form suggested for data analysis requires the researcher to log:

- the *data sets* in which the analysis was conducted;
- the *procedural steps*;
- the *decision rules* used to manage the data;

- the *analysis operations* involved;
- the preliminary *conclusions* to which the analysis led.

A completed set of forms would enable an external auditor to follow an audit trail more easily and thus more quickly assess the accuracy and legitimacy of the procedures used. The act of completing the forms is also useful for the evaluator since it helps to systematise the whole conduct of an evaluation.

The employment of an external auditor is likely to be justified only in the case of substantial and well resourced evaluations. However, the kind of approach outlined above is relevant to time-constrained evaluation for at least three reasons. First, as Lincoln and Guba observe:

> Naturalistic criteria of trustworthiness are open-ended; they can never be satisfied to such an extent that the trustworthiness of the inquiry could be labelled as unassailable. This fact stands in marked contrast to that of conventional enquiry . . . . The conventional inquirer who can demonstrate that he or she has randomised or controlled all confounding variables, selected a probability sample that is representative of a defined population, replicated the study (or those parts of it that are concerned with instruments), and secured intersubjective agreement can claim absolute trustworthiness – the inquiry is, within that closed system, utterly unassailable. One is *compelled* to accept its trustworthiness. But naturalistic inquiry operates as an *open* system; no amount of member checking, triangulation, persistent observation, auditing, or whatever can ever compel; it can at best *persuade*.
>
> (Lincoln and Guba, 1985: 329)

Assailability will be even more likely for time-constrained evaluation which requires the abbreviation, modification or even the omission of some of the methods and trustworthiness criteria which may be feasible in more substantial and lengthy naturalistic evaluations. In an essentially positivist culture, such evaluations will be particularly prone to the charge that they are not scientific. This is a charge frequently made against the findings of HMI and other inspectorates. It should, of course, be noted that a close examination of most of the research and evaluation which do claim to be scientific shows that they too fail to meet many of the criteria of the positivist paradigm. For example, drawing truly random samples of subjects from defined populations is notoriously difficult to achieve in educational research. The claim to absolute unassailability is actually rarely justified in practice. That aside, however, the fact remains that naturalistic-style evaluations will be particularly vulnerable to being considered untrustworthy.

It is therefore only by scrupulously recording their methods, criteria and decision rules that naturalistic evaluators in general, and time-constrained evaluators in particular, can be in a position to refute such a charge. Evaluators need to be able to demonstrate, if and when challenged, how their findings are grounded in relevant data and derived from systematic and rational procedures.

Evaluations might be judged less in terms of an idealised positivist paradigm – one which, moreover, has proved vulnerable even within the once confident citadel of the hard sciences – and more as examples of systematic investigations. In other words, sceptics might reasonably ask an evaluator such questions as: What evidence have you got? How did you collect it? And crucially: How did you use the evidence to arrive at that conclusion? The sceptics should then ask themselves: Am I persuaded by these answers? Is there any other evidence around, which we or others possess, which may be regarded as better, truer or more complete than that of the evaluators?

A second reason for the relevance of auditing lies in its significance for permanent evaluation teams such as national or local inspectorates. Inspectorates will increasingly assume a higher profile as the practice of inspection spreads and becomes more commonplace. It is extremely likely therefore that inspection will come under closer scrutiny than hitherto. Inspectorates will need to convince both practitioners and the public that they use methods and procedures which are systematic and worthy of confidence. This will require inspectorates making their *modus operandi* explicit, and demonstrating the dependability and confirmability of evaluation findings by an internal auditing process supplemented by the occasional external audit. Inspectorates will also find it useful in maintaining their credibility to publish details of the training programme for new recruits and for experienced staff. A significant element of the training programme would be concerned with the acquisition, retention and further development of evaluation and auditing skills.

The third reason for emphasising the auditing model lies in the likely growth of self-evaluation along the lines suggested in chapter 3. Self-evaluation will increasingly be an exercise of short duration as it is incorporated as a regularly recurring feature into the annual budget and planning cycles of institutions. The approach and methods of time-constrained evaluation are as relevant to internal or self-evaluation as to external evaluation. Governing bodies, employers and local communities will no doubt demand reassurance that internal reviews and evaluations are critical, rigorous, useful and worthy of belief. The LEAs themselves are well placed to provide that reassurance by deploying their inspectorates, for part of their time, as external auditors of the evaluation activities of schools and colleges.

THE ROLE OF JUDGEMENT

Reference has already been made to the list of aspects which HMI regularly includes in its inspection visits. Assessments typically take the form of a short piece of descriptive and evaluative text and a rating on a five point scale. It is assumed that the resulting text and rating are influenced by a series of prompts which indicate the kind of attributes that may be looked for when describing a particular aspect. Similar loose frameworks of judgement are used by other inspectorates (see Figure 8.2).

These frameworks tend to conform to the same basic implicit structure which is shown in Figure 9.1. In this example X represents 'quality of pupil learning in a lesson'. A, B, C represent the main general attributes of the aspect X under consideration. Attribute C in the example is 'organisation of the lesson'. For ease of representation it is assumed that X is defined by three attributes only. In reality some Xs will be defined by two attributes, others by three or more. Each attribute is split into sub-attributes. The number of sub-attributes needed will vary. Again for simplicity each attribute is shown split into three sub-attributes, for example, C into C_x, C_y and C_z. C_y is 'formulation of clear objectives'. It is unusual for

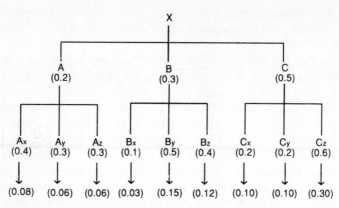

Figure 9.1 Idealised model of judgement

the attributes to be of equal importance in determining the condition of X. Let us suppose that an individual inspector assigns a weight to each attribute to represent its relative degree of importance as factors of 1. Figure 9.1 shows the result: A = 0.2, B = 0.3, C = 0.5. These are referred to as *normalised* weightings.

As with attributes, each sub-attribute now needs to have a weight assigned, again as a factor of 1. In our example the three sub-attributes of A have been assigned weights as follows: A_x = 0.4, A_y = 0.3, A_z = 0.3. To find the weighting of each sub-attribute in relation to the main aspect under review, X, it is necessary to multiply the weighting of the attribute by the weighting of the sub-attribute. Thus the weighting of A_x is 0.2 multiplied by 0.4 = 0.08. Since the whole structure is tree-like, the attributes may be thought of as branches and the sub-attributes as twigs. The final weights for each twig have been obtained by 'multiplying through the tree'.

Let us suppose that the inspector visits a particular lesson and wishes to make an assessment of X. He may decide to rate the lesson on the attributes and he will do this on a five point scale, with 1 denoting a situation with many good features and 5 a generally poor situation, one with many shortcomings. If he does not feel able to make global ratings on any or all of the three attributes, he will rate the sub-attributes. In Figure 9.2 it is assumed that he rates the sub-attributes throughout.

192

	NORMALISED WEIGHTING (NW)	RATING (R)	(NW) x (R)
A_x	0.08	3	0.24
A_y	0.06	2	0.12
A_z	0.06	4	0.24
B_x	0.03	1	0.03
B_y	0.15	3	0.45
B_z	0.12	1	0.12
C_x	0.10	1	0.10
C_y	0.10	2	0.20
C_z	0.30	4	1.20
OVERALL RATING			2.7

Figure 9.2 Ratings for model in Figure 9.1

The normalised weighting for each sub-attribute, A_x, A_y and so on, has been repeated in the first column, the rating on the five point scale is given in the second column and their product in the third. The total product gives the overall rating. In this example it is evident that the overall assessment of X is 'marginally below average'. It is also easy to make other observations, merely by inspection. Three sub-attribute ratings B_x, B_z and C_x attract the top rating and the weightings show that, of these, two are considered quite important elements within the assessment, while one, B_x, is of little importance. Of the two with the low rating of 4, C_z has the highest normalised rating of all and its score in the last column is highly significant in pulling down the overall rating. The inspector can readily see, and therefore communicate to the teacher of the lesson, both where the strengths lie and what aspect of the quality of pupil learning requires the closest attention. One final observation: had the inspector decided to rate for B and C the sub-attributes but for A only the whole attribute, giving it a rating of 3, the overall rating would be unchanged. The sum of NW x R for A_x, A_y and A_z is 0.6, identical with the product of the NW for A (0.2) and the R of 3.

The model outlined above has been derived from the approach to evaluation developed by Edwards and Newman (1982). This has generally been employed for macro-comparative evaluations, concerned particularly with social programmes, policy issues and management decisions. However, the basic model may also be applicable to judgements made at the kind of micro-level represented by Figure 9.1.

The model in Figure 9.1 is built on a number of assumptions:

- complex aspects can be analysed into a limited set of independent attributes;
- these attributes can be further analysed into a potential hierarchy of independent sub-attributes;
- global judgements on particular aspects can be made by linear combinations of the separate weighted assessments made on each constituent attribute.

These assumptions generate essentially a *logical* model of judgement. Different assumptions, that judgements are made configurally rather than linearly, would yield different models. Moreover, there is no guarantee that Figure 9.1 represents an appropriate *psychological* model, that it adequately accounts for what goes on in the head when a judgement is made. In fact we seem to know very little about the processes involved in making judgements on complex issues. However, judgements *are* made. In particular, inspectors make judgements. Furthermore, they regularly make judgements involving the rating of complex entities. Such ratings have the apparent advantage of condensing a judgement, the expression of which might otherwise require a lengthy description, into a single rating. Another advantage is that separate ratings, made of different instances of the same class of phenomenon, can be aggregated to provide more generalised descriptive judgements. As already noted, this is a significant development pioneered by HMI. By aggregating the ratings contained in the notes of visit of HM inspectors throughout the country, it is possible to produce such authoritative pronouncements as:

> The greatest change has been in the quality of oral work, 60% of lessons are now judged satisfactory, compared with 40% in the recent cycle of inspections.
>
> (DES, 1989c: para 14)

This is a quotation from the report on *Standards in education 1987–8*. The 60 per cent of lessons referred to were those seen by HMI in secondary schools during 1987–8 which were graded 1, 2 or 3 on the five point scale. This figure is compared to the percentage of lessons similarly graded over the period 1982–6 (DES, 1988c: para 66). The figure for these earlier years was 40 per cent.

The fact is, however, that we do not know exactly how HMI, or indeed other inspectorates, make this kind of judgement. How do inspectors put together in their heads the various pieces of evidence which ultimately issue as a judgemental rating? How dependable are the ratings made by individual inspectors? How is judgement nurtured and developed? The purpose of outlining the model in Figure 9.1 is not to offer it as a definitive explanation of inspectorial judgement but to present it as a provisional but customarily neglected framework for examining an important topic.

Inspectors, by dint of working together regularly as permanent teams, have the opportunity, denied to the occasional evaluator, to develop individual and collective judgements which are credible, dependable and confirmable. This will not be realised, however, without a serious investment of time in a sustained training and development programme, such as the one below.

Programme for developing team judgements

1 Agree within the team the kind of broad aspects of education which should be the subject of regular assessment.
2 Identify the main attributes which constitute the aspects chosen. Explore the extent to which the attributes for particular aspects need to be differentiated.
3 Experiment in assigning weights to the attributes. Seek to achieve consensus on attribute weightings between inspectors.
4 Develop a rating scale and agree operational definitions for each point on the scale.
5 Practise applying attribute weightings and ratings to give global assessments on the aspects chosen. Practise, where possible in pairs or small groups, in the field or using suitable video substitutes. Determine the extent of consistency between the ratings of individual inspectors.
6 Revise attributes and weightings as necessary.
7 Incorporate procedures in normal inspection programme.
8 Maintain occasional individual and group consistency checks.

To date, few inspectorates seem to have recognised the crucial importance of establishing systematic programmes for developing individual and collective judgements. They will need to do so if they are to survive in a climate in which expertise rather than ascribed authority is increasingly seen as the basis for credibility.

REPORTING TIME-CONSTRAINED EVALUATIONS

Institutions and programmes are not static entities: they change, on occasions quite rapidly. This can pose a problem for evaluation. The time lag between completing an evaluation and reporting can be such that the outcomes are no longer appropriate to the evaluand. All evaluations therefore risk the possibility of becoming historical irrelevancies – at least for potential users of the information produced. Time-constrained evaluation is explicitly concerned with serving the *specific* information requirements of users. Its outcomes need to be reported as soon after the completion of the evaluation as possible. This requirement is met to some extent by the frequent practice of presenting the conclusions orally at the end of the evaluation. This, as already noted, is an example of the trustworthiness technique of member-checking. It also provides a further opportunity for the evaluator to consider any additional views of the evaluatees as well as their reactions to the specific conclusions reported. However, oral presentations cannot be a complete substitute for the final formal report, which should be produced within a fortnight of the completion of the evaluation.

It is recognised that this is quite a stringent aim which is seldom achieved. The notion of time-constrained evaluation as a distinctive approach to enquiry is based on two fundamental principles, that evaluations: are carried out swiftly; are reported on promptly. Previous chapters have offered suggestions for the first of these principles. The answer to the second lies in part in clarifying the nature of the stance to be taken on several important issues:

- the scope of the evaluation;
- the information needs of users and stakeholders;
- thick versus thin description;

- substantive versus methodological content;
- the format of reports.

The scope of the evaluation

The potential complexity of an evaluation report – and therefore, to an extent, the time taken on its production – depends on the scope of the evaluation. The quantity of the data collected, and the ramifications for subsequent analysis and interpretation, will generally be greater in the case of the evaluation of an institution or major programme than in that of a department. A longer time interval for the appearance of reports from such cases may be justified.

The main concern of this book, however, is not with large-scale, relatively protracted, research-oriented evaluations. Instead, the emphasis has been upon the potentially much more numerous, short evaluations which are embedded within the day-by-day management concerns of systems and institutions. This type of evaluation is essential if the organisation of education and training is to conform to the avowed ideal of rational management. Time-constrained evaluation, being geared to the specific and relatively urgent information requirements of actual users, has little room for reports which are not produced promptly.

The information needs of users and stakeholders

Time-constrained evaluation is unequivocally determined by the information needs of users and the concerns of stakeholders. These needs must be clear before an evaluation proceeds. The crucial question to users must be: What kind of information, not available to you at present, would significantly change what you do in relation to the evaluand? A comparable acid-test question to stakeholders, who may be distinct from users, is: In carrying out the proposed evaluation in order to provide users with required information, what issues and concerns is it essential, in your view, to consider? The answers to both questions must be thought through and expressed precisely before an evaluation can be justified. Clear-cut answers to these questions effectively define the objectives of an evaluation. They enable a report to be written swiftly, since only a little time is spent deciding what to include and in what form. If information needs and issues are clearly formulated, any subsequent report will almost write itself.

Since the information needs of particular users and stakeholders may sometimes differ, a case might be made for having a different report for each distinguishable group. However, the existence of different reports may give rise to the suspicion that information is being deliberately withheld, in order perhaps to keep certain groups in the dark. In most cases therefore it is better to produce a single report. Indeed it may be argued that an important educative function is served if each group knows of the information needs and concerns of others.

Thick versus thin description

Conventional evaluation reports, particularly those that are based on a case study approach, are often rich in thick description. Thick description typically includes extensive quotations from interview data and detailed portrayals of the activities, situations and often the personalities associated with the case study. Thick description will facilitate the transferability of the findings of the case study. However, as noted previously, transferability is not a primary concern of individual time-constrained evaluations. Instead, the aim is to provide a service to specific users and stakeholders. Reports should therefore set out, as clearly and precisely as possible, the information requirements of these two groups. Reports will tend therefore to be characterised by thin rather than thick descriptions, by depersonalised rather than personalised accounts. Thus, although it is virtually impossible to write a report without referring implicitly to the influence of individuals, there should be no attempt to depict roles in the kind of graphic detail favoured by some case study writers.

Substantive versus methodological content

Evaluation reports are often modelled on those produced for research studies. For these, details are usually given of the design adopted, the methods and instruments used, the nature of the data collected and the techniques of analysis which have been applied. In addition to these methodological details, research-style reports will be concerned with the substantive content of findings, interpretation, recommendations and implications. In the case of reports of time-constrained evaluation, given their avowedly user-information orientation, the main emphasis should be on substantive content. Only the briefest details of methodology, such as a list of the main sources of data and some indication of sample characteristics, will normally be necessary. The important point is that the information presented in a report should be unambiguously clear to the potential user and not risk being obscured by what may be seen as a clutter of methodological concerns.

However, while methodological details may largely be omitted from a report, it is important that they be accessible if required by users. For example, the evaluator may be asked to justify a particular piece of information, evaluative description or recommendation contained in the report. In order to do so, the evaluator must have the data and its analysis appropriately organised and ready to hand.

The format of reports

The argument throughout this chapter has been that the reports of time-constrained evaluation should be brief, a point well made by Caldwell and Spinks (1988). Referring to the role played by evaluation in their approach to collaborative school management, they comment:

> It is therefore necessary that the results and recommendations [of evaluation] are reported in an effective and efficient manner. This need is often neglected in evaluation work and lengthy reports are prepared which explain in fine detail the methods employed and information gathered. The recipient often fails to reach the recommendations at the end. This leads to frustration for all concerned, especially those who prepared the report. There is a need to document the actual work involved in the evaluation, but it only needs to be available if requested. What is required immediately is a short, succinct report that effectively summarises the findings of the evaluation group and highlights recommendations for future action.
>
> (Caldwell and Spinks, 1988: 153–4)

They argue that even what they refer to as major evaluations of school programmes should be written up in the form of two-page reports. Such reports would consist of:

- an *introduction*: a paragraph or so mentioning the main evaluation methods used;
- a succinct list of the *inadequacies* and *problem areas identified*;
- a brief description of the *successful outcomes of the programme*;
- a concluding *summary and set of recommendations*.

This criterion of extreme economy for report writing, although recommended to those involved in evaluation as part of a total approach to school management, could also be extended beneficially to other contexts. Many years of experience of reading reports produced by academic evaluators lead me to say that they are invariably too long and generally not in forms suitable for busy educationists to use. It is unrealistic to expect practitioners to have the same motivation, commitment and time to read lengthy research-style reports as academics may have. One of the promising developments within the TSAS is a conscious attempt to produce short and action-specific reports on inspections of YT.

Length and readability are important aspects of the more general issue of the format of reports. Reports are invariably cast in the format of narrative text. Now narrative text, particularly if lengthy, jargon-ridden and not consciously structured for the needs of its audience, may be a very inefficient mode of communicating the outcomes of evaluation studies. Surprisingly few serious attempts have been made to experiment with alternative formats.

One of the problems of narrative text is that it is necessarily sequential. As a result, the ability to see connections between different elements of a study and discern important outcomes and implications may require frequent cross-checking and referral back within the text. In addition, text may impose heavy demands on the information processing capacity of the reader. The use of diagrammatic representations may be helpful. The advantages are that they combine the virtue of brevity with the opportunity of seeing connections at a glance. Figure 9.3 provides an example.

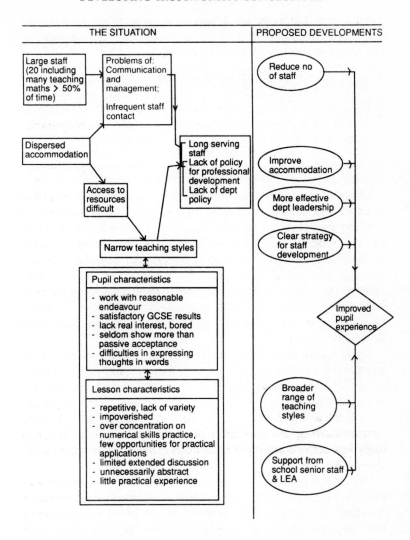

Figure 9.3 **The findings of an evaluation of a mathematics department**

CONCLUDING NOTE

The argument presented in this chapter can be briefly stated. Time-constrained evaluation results in the formulation of conclusions and judgements which are: regarded as trustworthy; user and information oriented; produced speedily; and reported succinctly.

10

CONCLUSION AND SUMMARY

EVALUATION AND RATIONAL PLANNING

Perhaps the most significant of recent government initiatives in education and training has been the attempt to implement systematically and comprehensively a rational planning model. Although there are variants of the model, the differences between them are largely ones of terminology. Strategic plans, corporate plans, development plans and business plans are some of the names used to describe the several manifestations of the model. At heart the model is concerned with four basic functions which constitute an interactive cycle:

- determining what an organisation shall do by formulating priorities and objectives;
- translating these into operational plans, each of which is defined in terms of more detailed objectives;
- systematically assessing whether the plans have been implemented economically, efficiently and effectively;
- using the results of the assessment to adjust, modify or change the plan; and provide a basis for determining the next phase of the planning cycle.

The third function is that of evaluation, and in particular what is normally referred to as programme evaluation.

Previous attempts to incorporate evaluation as an integral part of the organisation and delivery of education and training have generally been patchy and of limited impact and utility. Part of the reason for this lay in a pervasive management culture in which evaluation was not seen as an essential requirement of rational planning. That situation is already changing, as the planning model increasingly penetrates the system at all levels – from the LEA and TEC to the institution and individual programme and project. The model is also locked into place, in a way that was not possible before, by linking it to the crucial issue of resource provision through such devices as LMS.

SOME EVALUATION PROPOSITIONS

It is in the above context that the arguments presented in the previous chapters have been developed. In brief, these arguments can be summarised in terms of a number of propositions which, in the case of the education system, can be represented as follows:

- An LEA should have a comprehensive evaluation strategy and programme.
- This should be derived from the strategic plan of the LEA.
- The evaluation programme should be planned in advance, with the allocation of appropriate resources clearly identified, and organised on an annual rolling basis.
- Key elements of the programme include the monitoring and evaluation of institutions and major programmes and projects.
- The programme will normally be composed of contributions from external evaluators, inspectors and officers, institutional self-evaluation and performance indicators. It will also take account of any inspection activities of HMI within the LEA.
- The evaluation programme is a source of educational information and knowledge which claims to be trustworthy. It is a major contributor to the formal information system of the LEA.
- Individual evaluations are unequivocally geared to the provision of specific information required by key users as a basis for action.
- A major part of the programme will consist of evaluations carried out under conditions of time-constraint.
- Evaluation, the provision of information and their joint relationship to strategic planning are key features of a wider commitment to total quality management.

The propositions can also be translated to fit the micro-level of the institution or individual programme. For example, the school or college development plan is the equivalent of the strategic plan at the LEA level. An institution's evaluation programme should be related to the development plan and should include activities of internal review and audit.

Although these propositions are framed specifically in terms of LEAs, they are also generally relevant to TECs. The relationship between a TEC and its training providers is analogous in some ways to that between an LEA and its institutions. The development of an evaluation strategy and programme along the above lines is wholly consistent with the strategic planning model proposed for the TECs.

Embedding evaluation as an integral part of the planning process ensures that accountability, a frequently cited justification for evaluation, becomes a specific and realistic requirement rather than one which is diffuse and vaguely menacing. If systems, institutions and programmes are to account for what goes on in their name, this is best attained through the provision of reliable information about the progress and outcomes of plans and developments.

TIME-CONSTRAINED EVALUATION

The commitment to TCE is a consequence of two factors in particular. First, the potential number of evaluations needed is such that only a few could be resourced realistically on the scale typified in the evaluation literature, those which may be referred to as protracted or research-style evaluations. Second, protracted evaluations are unlikely to provide the specific information necessary to satisfy the short-term and frequently changing requirements of managers and practitioners. An approach is therefore suggested in which evaluation resources of personnel and time are concentrated to give a series of short evaluations.

The argument has not been that TCE is the only approach to evaluation but rather that it necessarily occupies a central role in a total evaluation strategy and programme. Certainly, at the LEA or TEC level there is a continuing place for systematic evaluations, particularly for major policy or development initiatives.

The concept of TCE developed in chapters 6 to 9 can be

summed up tersely as evaluation carried out quickly and reported on promptly and succinctly. It can be understood more fully in terms of the following broad assertions:

- It is related to the general traditions of fieldwork enquiry and qualitative research. It therefore draws on the methods of data collection, analysis and interpretation associated with these traditions.
- It is sympathetic to a view of evaluation which sees the main task as the achievement of more informed consensual constructions for all users and stakeholders.
- It recognises that judgement is necessarily involved at every stage of an evaluation and thus cannot be eliminated by the use of either more sophisticated methods of data collection or more refined methods of analysis. Rather the task is to make explicit the basis on which judgements are made and to develop the capacity to make increasingly discriminating and trustworthy judgements.
- Carrying out evaluations within substantially reduced time-scales requires some modification of the methods and procedures normally used in more extensive studies.
- Trustworthiness is ultimately assessed by external scrutiny of the evaluation process. The essential question is whether the conduct of the evaluation represents a disciplined and systematic enquiry in which the information generated follows logically from the methods and procedures adopted.

Implications of TCE

Inspectorates

Although not usually recognised as such, inspection is an example of *de facto* time-constrained evaluation. However, despite its familiarity and long history, surprisingly little has been written about the methodological basis of inspection. Indeed inspection appears to be methodologically vacuous. As the practice of inspection becomes less exclusively associated with the prestige, authority and mystique of HMI and spreads to LEAs, it is likely to come under close scrutiny. This will be particularly the case if the findings of inspection are made available in the public domain. Inspectorates will therefore need to be able to make explicit their methodological credentials in a way in which few are able to do at the present time. Listed below are some of the anticipated implications for an inspectorate.

- Development of a handbook on inspection based on the methods and procedures of TCE.
- Preparation of a shorter version of the handbook for circulation to institutional or programme staff in advance of an inspection.
- Systematic training programmes in TCE for both new and experienced inspectors.
- Regular checks conducted to ensure that, where criteria, categories and codes have been agreed, they are used consistently by individual inspectors.
- All data pertaining to inspections, including in particular the written-up field notes, and details and examples of the data analytic techniques used, to be retained: as an inspection record to which reference can be made if queries are raised subsequently; as a basis for use as a potential audit trail.
- Occasional external audit of the inspection process using a properly documented audit trail.
- Brief details of inspection procedures to be publicly available, in the form of a short booklet or pamphlet, as evidence of the inspectorate's credibility.
- Development of, and training in, procedures for auditing the time-constrained self-evaluations carried out by the staff of institutions or programmes.

An inspectorate should be particularly well placed to become skilled in TCE. This is because inspectors form relatively close-knit groups, likely to be engaged on inspections on a regular basis. They will therefore have many opportunities to compare notes, check out their respective perceptions of situations and develop consensual constructions relevant to such issues as the quality of educational experience.

It is a matter of some regret that these opportunities do not seem to have been very firmly grasped in the past – at least by LEA inspectorates and advisory services. There are probably two principal reasons for this. First, inspectorates have tended to reflect a culture based on the idea of the talented, autonomous individualist rather than of the corporate team working, where possible, within a common set of educational values.

Second, the culture has not generally been one in which there was a strong empathy with the traditions of evaluation or the methodological disciplines of systematic fieldwork. However, both of these characteristics are disappearing fast and LEA inspectorates are already looking quite different from those which existed before the ERA.

Institutional self-evaluation

The goal of evaluating every institution annually is not feasible. Under an inspection programme alone the time between successive evaluations of an institution may be as much as five to ten years. Self-evaluation is the only realistic way of ensuring an annual evaluation cycle. In the past, however, self-evaluation has been difficult to implement on a regular and comprehensive basis. This has been due principally to two factors:

- A tendency to attempt the evaluation of the total institution in a single exercise rather than adopting a rolling programme over several years.
- A general vagueness about what aspects to evaluate and for what purpose.

Both of these difficulties are overcome by relating evaluation specifically to the institutional development plan. This will be expressed in terms of different priorities and plans for each annual cycle. As a result, it can be expected that most, if not all, of the main areas and activities of the institution will be covered over a reasonable period of years. Focusing in any year on a limited number of priorities and programmes, and the individual targets associated with these, makes evaluation a realistic task and avoids a situation where much time is spent deciding exactly what to assess. However, even with this phased approach to self-evaluation, institutional staff will not generally have sufficient time at their disposal to carry out substantial systematic evaluations. In other words, TCE is as much a necessity for institutional staff involved in self-evaluation as it is for inspectors.

However, the establishment of evaluation as an integral part of the process of development planning by institutional and programme staff will not occur spontaneously and uniformly without leadership from the LEA or the TEC. Some of the important preconditions for successful implementation include:

- Agreement on a general framework and format for self-evaluation for use by institutions and programmes, including a handbook on the application of time-constrained methods.
- Training for all staff on TCE. This is a substantial task and would need to be maintained as a permanent feature of the training programme of the LEA or TEC. This is to ensure that new staff are inducted into the system and that existing staff have regular opportunities for updating their skills.
- Inclusion of an appropriate element in the initial training of teachers and trainers.
- Maintenance of a documented record of the process and outcomes of self-evaluation as an audit trail.
- Development of a procedure by which inspectors audit self-evaluations.

It could be argued that, in the ideal world, self-evaluation alone would be sufficient and that inspectorates would become redundant; but there are at least two problems with this argument. First, oversight by inspectors may be necessary to attest to the trustworthiness of self-evaluations; and, second, even where self-evaluations can be accepted with confidence, it is unlikely that results could be effectively aggregated to give information of comparable dependability to that provided by local and national inspectorates. Inspectorates are likely, therefore, to be required for some time to come as key contributors to comprehensive evaluation strategies.

Quality assurance

Growing interest has been shown of late in quality assurance as a means of clarifying the functions and organisation of education and training. The concept of quality assurance has several important implications for the role of evaluation.

- The prime emphasis of quality assurance on the *customer* would suggest the importance of collecting student/trainee views of their courses. This tends to be neglected in many institutional and programme evaluations.

- The idea of the *supplier–customer chain* – that everyone in an organisation is both a supplier and a customer – would broaden the traditional emphasis of evaluation to include the effects of middle and senior management on teacher performance, and thus indirectly on student performance.
- The identification of the course as *product* would also help to ensure that evaluation did not concentrate exclusively on the performance of teacher and students but on the total context.
- The emphasis on *internal reviews* would favour a self-evaluation approach, while also indicating the important requirement for independent auditing.

Inspectors as external auditors

If inspectors are to spend part of their time in the future as auditors of the internal evaluation and review processes of institutions, four requirements are necessary:

- Inspectors should be independent of the institutions being audited. This may mean forgoing any close advisory or developmental relationship with individual institutions.
- An acceptable range of methods and procedures should be used by those in institutions for carrying out internal reviews and evaluations.
- The process and the outcomes of these activities should be systematically recorded by institutional staff.
- Inspectors should use agreed procedures for conducting audits.

TCE, as outlined here, provides a general framework for carrying out the second of these requirements and, to some extent, the third and fourth as well.

CONCLUDING NOTE

It is crucial that the 1990s become the decade where high-quality evaluation is, for the first time, an integral and influential part of the provision of education and training. This book is a contribution towards fulfilling that aspiration by setting out how individual evaluations can be realistically conducted within a system-wide programme. In addition, the book seeks to unify what seems at first glance to be a diverse and disparate set of concepts: monitoring, evaluation, inspection, performance indicators, self-evaluation, quality assurance and accountability. The focus of the unification is the practical approach of time-constrained evaluation.

REFERENCES

Audit Commission (1989a) *Assuring Quality in Education*, London: HMSO.

Audit Commission (1989b) *Losing an Empire, Finding a Role: The LEA of the Future*, London: HMSO.

Baker, K. (1988) *Secretary of State's Speech to SEO*, 22 January 1988, London: Press Office DES.

Barnes, D., Johnson, G., Jordan, S., Layton, D., Medway, E. and Yeomans, D. (1987) *The TVEI Curriculum 14–16: An Interim Case Study Based on Case Studies in Twelve Schools*, Sheffield: MSC.

Becher, T., Eraut, M. and Knight, J. (1978) *Accountability in Education*, Windsor: NFER Nelson.

Beeby, C. E. (1977) 'The Meaning of Evaluation', in: *Current Issues in Education* (4), Wellington: Department of Education, 68–78.

Blackie, J. (1970) *Inspecting and the Inspectorate*, London: Routledge & Kegan Paul.

Blackie, J. (1982) 'HM Inspectorate of Schools 1839–1966', in: McCormick, R. and Nuttall, D. L. (eds) (1982) *Curriculum Evaluation & Assessment in Educational Institutions*, Block 2, Part 3, Milton Keynes: Open University Press, 7–13.

Bogdan, R. C. and Biklen, S. K. (1982) *Qualitative Research for Education*, London: Allyn & Bacon.

Bolam R., Smith G. and Canter, H. (1978) *LEA Advisers and the Mechanisms of Innovation*, Windsor: NFER Nelson.

Broadfoot, P., James, M., McMeekings, S., Nuttall, D. and Stierer, B. (1988) *Records of Achievement*, Report of the National Evaluation of Pilot Schemes, London: HMSO.

Browne, S. (1979) 'The Accountability of HM Inspectorate (England)', in: Lello, J. (ed.) (1979) *Accountability in Education*, London: Ward Lock, 35–44.

BSI (1987a) *BS 5750 Quality Systems*, London: British Standards Institution.

BSI (1987b) *BS 4778 Quality Vocabulary* Part 1, London: British Standards Institution.

Burgess, R. G. (1982) *Field Research: A Source Book and Field Manual*, London: Allen & Unwin.

Caldwell, B. J. and Spinks, J. M. (1988) *The Self-managing School*, London: Falmer.

Chamier, A. (1989) 'The Role, Organization and Priorities of LEAs' Inspection and Advisory Services', paper presented at Peat Marwick McClintock/NFER Conference on *Assuring Quality and Developing Practice: The New LEA Role for the 1990s*, London.

CIPFA (1984) *Performance Indicators in the Education Service*, London: The Chartered Institute of Public Finance and Accountancy.

CIPFA (1988) *Performance Indicators for Schools*, London: The Chartered Institute of Public Finance and Accountancy.

Clift, P. (1981) 'LEA Schemes for School Self-Evaluation', paper presented at the Annual Conference of the *British Educational Research Association*, Crewe: 1–3 September 1981.

Clift, P. S., Nuttall, D. L. and McCormick, R. (1987) *Studies in School Self-Evaluation*, London: Falmer.

Cronbach, L. J., Ambron, S. R., Dornbusch, S. M., Hess, R. D., Hornik, R. C., Phillips, D. C., Walker, D. E. and Weiner, S. S. (1980) *Toward Reform of Program Evaluation*, San Francisco: Jossey-Bass.

Davidson, G. and Parsons, C. (1990) 'Evaluating Teaching as Learning Styles in TVEI', in: Hopkins, D. (ed.) (1990) *TVEI at the Change of Life*, Clevedon: Multilingual Matters, 50–64.

Dean, J. (1990) 'Inspecting Schools: An Educational Digest', *Education*, 16 March 1990.

Delbecq, A. L., Van de Ven, A. H. and Gustafson, D. H. (1975) *Group Techniques for Program Planning*, Illinois: Scott, Foresman & Co.

DES (1979) *Aspects of Secondary Education in England: A Survey by HMI*, London: HMSO.

DES (1985) *A Draft Statement on the Role of Local Education Authority Advisory Services*, London: DES.

DES (1986a) *Reporting Inspections: Maintained Schools*, London: DES.

DES (1986b) *Better Schools: Evaluation and Appraisal*, London: DES.

DES (1987) *Report by Her Majesty's Inspectorate on LEA Provision for Education and the Quality of Response in Schools and Colleges in England 1986*, London: DES.

DES (1988a) *Education Reform Act: Local Management of Schools*, circular 7/88, London: DES.

DES (1988b) *Education Support Grant*, draft circular, London: DES.

DES (1988c) *Secondary Schools: An Appraisal by HMI*, London: HMSO.

DES (1989a) *The Education (School Curriculum and Related Information) Regulations*, circular 14/89, London: DES.

DES (1989b) *School Indicators for Internal Management: An Aide Mémoire*, Publications Despatch Centre, London: DES.

DES (1989c) *Standards in Education 1987–88: A Report by HM Inspectorate*, London: DES.

DES/WO (1982) *Study of HM Inspectorate in England and Wales* (Rayner Report), London: HMSO.

DES/WO (1987) *Managing Colleges Efficiently*, report of a study of efficiency in non-advanced Further Education for the government and local authority associations, London: HMSO.

Ebbutt, D. (1988) 'Multi-site Case Study: Some Recent Practice and the Problems of Generalisation', *Cambridge Journal of Education*, 18(3), 347–63.

Edwards, W. and Newman, J. R. (1982) *Multi-attribute Evaluation*, London: Sage.

Elliott, J. (1980) 'Who Should Monitor Performance in Schools?', in: Sockett, H. (ed.) (1980) *Accountability in the English Educational System*, London: Hodder & Stoughton, 74–84.

Elliott, J. and Ebbutt, D. (1986) 'How do Her Majesty's Inspectors Judge Educational Quality?', *Curriculum*, 7(3), 130–40.

Ellis, R. (ed.) (1988) *Professional Competence and Quality Assurance in the Caring Professions*, London: Croom Helm.

Fitz-Gibbon, C. T. (1986) 'The Roles of the TVEI Local Evaluator', in: Hopkins, D. (ed.) (1986) *Evaluating TVEI: Some Methodological Issues*, Cambridge: Cambridge Institute of Education, 18–30.

Fitz-Gibbon, C. T. (1989) 'Using Performance Indicators: Educational Considerations', in: Levacic, R. (ed.) (1989) *Financial Management in Education*, Milton Keynes: Open University Press, 199–213.

Fitz-Gibbon, C. T. (1990) 'An Up-and-Running Indicator System', in: Fitz-Gibbon, C. T. (ed.) (1990) *Performance Indicators*, BERA Dialogues 2, Clevedon: Multilingual Matters, 88–95.

Flanders, N. A. (1970) *Analyzing Teacher Behaviour*, New York: Addison-Wesley.

Froggatt, B. (1988) 'A Small Scale Evaluation of Negotiated Learning', *SERCH*, 10, 8–11, City of Sheffield Education Department.

Glaser, B. G. and Strauss, A. L. (1967) *The Discovery of Grounded Theory*, London: Weidenfeld & Nicolson.

Goldstein, H. (1984) 'The Methodology of School Comparisons', *Oxford Review of Education*, (10)1, 69–74.

Goldstein, H. and Cuttance, P. (1988) 'A Note on National Assessment and School Comparison', *Journal of Educational Policy*, 3(2), 197–202.

Gray, J. and Hannon, V. (1986) 'HMI's Interpretations of Schools' Exam Results', *Journal of Education Policy*, 1(1), 23–33.

Gray, J., Jesson, D. and Jones, B. (1986) 'The Search for a Fairer Way of Comparing Schools' Examination Results', *Research Papers in Education*, 1(2), 91–122.

Gray, J., Jesson, D. and Sime, N. (1990) 'Estimating Differences in the Examination Performances of Secondary Schools in Six LEAs: A Multi-Level Approach to School Effectiveness', *Oxford Review of Education*, 16(2), 137–57.

Guba, E. G. and Lincoln, Y. S. (1981) *Effective Evaluation*, London: Jossey-Bass.

Guba, E. G. and Lincoln, Y. S. (1989) *Fourth Generation Evaluation*, London: Sage.

Halpern, E. S. (1983) *Auditing Naturalistic Inquiries: The Development and Application of a Model*, Unpub. doctoral dissertation, Indiana University.

Hancock, D. (1988) 'Speech to the NAIEA Executive', reprinted as a supplement to *Perspective*, The Journal for Advisers and Inspectors, 5 July 1988.

Hargreaves, D. H., Hopkins, D., Leask, M., Connolly, J. and Robinson, P. (1989) *Planning for School Development: Advice to Governors, Headteachers and Teachers*, London: DES.

Harland, J. (1987) 'The New INSET: A Transformation Scene', *Journal of Educational Policy*, 2(3), 235–44.

Hazelwood, R. D. (1990) 'Attitudes as Performance Indicators', in: Fitz-Gibbon, C. T. (ed.) (1990) *Performance Indicators*, BERA Dialogues 2, Clevedon: Multilingual Matters, 72–76.

Helsby, G. (1990) 'TVEI Pilots in Profile', in: Hopkins, D. (ed.) (1990) *TVEI at the Change of Life*, Clevedon: Multilingual Matters, 73–84.

Hinckley, S. M., Pole, J. S., Sims, D. and Storey, S. M. (1987) *The TVEI Experience: Views from Teachers and Students*, Sheffield: MSC.

HMI (1988a) 'Rating Scales and HMI Exercises', *Working Instruction 27/87*, London: DES.

HMI (1988b) *Inspection and Reporting: Working Notes for HMI*, London: DES.

HMSO (1968) *Report on Education and Science: Part I Her Majesty's Inspectorate*, London: HMSO.

HMSO (1977) *Education in Schools: A Consultative Document*, Cmnd 6869, London: HMSO.

HMSO (1984) *Better Schools*, Cmnd 9469, London: HMSO.

HMSO (1988) *The Education Reform Act 1988*, London: HMSO.

Holsti, O. R. (1969) *Content Analysis for the Social Sciences and the Humanities*, Reading, MA: Addison-Wesley.

Hopkins, D., Bollington, R. and Hewitt, D. (1989) 'Growing up with Qualitative Research and Evaluation', *Evaluation and Research in Education*, 2(3), 1–20.

Hulme, G. (1989) 'Performance Evaluation and Performance Indicators for Schools', in: Levacic, R. (ed.) (1989) *Financial Management in Education*, Milton Keynes: Open University Press, 189–98.

Hutchinson, B., Hopkins, D. and Howard, J. (1988) 'The Problem of Validity in the Qualitative Evaluation of Categorically Funded Curriculum Development Projects', *Educational Research*, 30(1), 54–64.

ILEA (1977) *Keeping the School Under Review*, London: County Hall.

Inglis, F. (1985) *The Management of Ignorance*, Oxford: Blackwell.

James, M. (1981) 'School Initiated Self Evaluation and the Improvement of Educational Practice: Some Issues for Consideration', paper presented at the Annual Conference of the British Educational Research Association, Crewe: 1–3 September 1981.

Jamieson, I. (1990) 'Markets, Rules and Culture: TVEI and the Management of Change', in: Fitz-Gibbon, C. T. (ed.) (1990) *Performance Indicators*, Clevedon: Multilingual Matters, 130–8.

Kogan, M. (1986) *Education Accountability: An Analytic Overview*, London: Hutchinson.

Lawton, D. and Gordon, P. (1987) *HMI*, London: Routledge & Kegan Paul.

Lincoln, Y. S. and Guba, E. G. (1985) *Naturalistic Inquiry*, Beverley Hills: Sage.

Marder, J. V. and Johnson, J. R. V. (1988) *British Education Thesaurus*, Leeds: Leeds University Press.

McCabe,C. (1990) 'Evaluating TVEI: What We Have Learned', in: Hopkins, D. (ed.) (1990) *TVEI at the Change of Life*, Clevedon: Multilingual Matters, 10–19.

McCormick, R. and Nuttall, D. L. (eds) (1982) *Curriculum Evaluation & Assessment in Educational Institutions*, Block 2, Part 3, Milton Keynes: Open University Press.

McCormick, R. and James, M. (1983) *Curriculum Evaluation in Schools*, London: Croom Helm.

McDonald, B. (1976) 'Evaluation and the Control of Education', in: Tawney, D. (ed.) (1976) *Curriculum Evaluation Today: Trends and Implications*, Schools Council Research Studies, London: Macmillan.

Miles, M. B. and Huberman, A. M. (1984) *Qualitative Data Analysis*, London: Sage.

MSC (1986) *Guide to Content and Quality on YTS/Approved Training Organisations*, Sheffield: Training Agency.

Murphy, K. and Henderson, S. (1988) *The Early Inspections: An Evaluation of the Training Standards Advisory Service*, Sheffield: Training Agency.

Nevo, D. (1986) 'Conceptualisation of Educational Evaluation', in: House, E. (ed.) (1986) *New Directions in Educational Evaluation*, Lewes: Falmer Press.

Nixon, J. (1989) 'Curriculum Evaluation: Old and New Paradigms', in: Entwistle, N. (ed.) (1989) *Handbook of Educational Ideas and Practices*, London: Routledge, 637–46.

Noblit, G. W. and Eaker, D. J. (1988) 'Evaluation Designs as Political Strategies', in: *Politics of Education Association Year Book 1988–9*, special issue of the *Journal of Educational Policy*, 3(5), 127–38.

Oakes, J. (1989) 'School Context and Organization', in: Shavelson, R. J. et al. (eds) (1989) *Indicators for Monitoring Mathematics and Science Education*, Santa Monica: Rand Co., 25–39.

Oakland, J. S. (1989) *Total Quality Management*, London: Heinemann.

Patton, M. Q. (1980) *Qualitative Evaluation Methods*, Beverly Hills: Sage.

Patton, M. Q. (1987) *Creative Evaluation*, London: Sage.

Pearce, J. (1986a) 'School Oversight in England and Wales', *European Journal of Education*, 21(4), 331–4.

Pearce, J. (1986b) *Standards and the LEA: The Accountability of Schools*, Windsor: NFER/Nelson.

Poster, C. and Poster, D. (1991) *Teacher Appraisal: a Guide to Training*, London: Routledge.

Ranson, S. (1988) 'From 1944 to 1988: Education, Citizenship and Democracy', *Local Government Studies*, 14 (1), 1–19.

Rhodes, G. (1981) *Inspectorates in British Government: Law Enforcement and Standards of Efficiency*, London: Allen & Unwin.

Ruddock, J. (1984) 'A Study in the Dissemination of Action Research', in: Burgess, R. G. (ed.) (1984) *The Research Process in Educational Settings*, London: Falmer Press 187–210.

Ruddock, J. (1985) 'A Case for Case Records?: A Discussion of Some Aspects of Lawrence Stenhouse's Work in Case Study Methodology', in: Burgess, R. G. (ed.) (1985) *Strategies of Educational Research*, London: Falmer Press, 101–19.

Saunders, M. (1986) 'Developing a Large Scale "Local" Evaluation of TVEI', in: Hopkins, D. (ed.) (1986) *Evaluating TVEI: Some Methodological Issues*, Cambridge: Cambridge Institute of Education, 41–51.

Scheerens, J. (1990) 'School Effectiveness Research and the Development of Process Indicators of School Functioning', *School Effectiveness and School Improvement*, 1(1), 61–80.

Shipman, M. (1979) *In-School Evaluation*, London: Heinemann.

Simons, H. (1987) *Getting to Know Schools in a Democracy*, London: Falmer Press.

Smith, P. (1987) 'Performance Indicators in the National Health Service', *Public Money*, 6(4), 35–9.

Stenhouse, L. (1982) 'The Conduct, Analysis, and Reporting of Case Study in Educational Research and Evaluation', in: McCormick, R. (ed.) (1982) *Calling Education to Account*, London: Heinemann, 261–73.

Stillman, A. B. (1988) 'LEA Advisers: Change and Management', *Educational Research* 30(3), 190–201.

Stillman, A. B. (1989) 'Institutional Evaluation and LEA Advisory Services', *Research Papers in Education*, 4(2), 3–27.

Stillman, A. B. and Grant, M. (1989) *The LEA Adviser – A Changing Role*, Windsor: NFER Nelson.

TA (1988) *Training Standards Advisory Service*, First Annual Report (1987/1988), Sheffield: Training Agency.

TA (1989a) *TVEI Programme Performance Indicators*, A Guide to Authorities for Annual Reviews Beginning September 1990, London: Training Agency.

TA (1989b) *TVEI Programme Performance Indicators*, Supplement to the Guide (for Annual Reviews Beginning September 1990), London: Training Agency.

TA (1989c) *TECs: Guide to Planning*, Sheffield: Training Agency.

Theodossin, E. and Thompson, C. (1987) 'Performance Indicators: Theory and Practice', *Coombe Lodge Report*, 20(1), 1–68.

Thomas, N. (1982) 'HM Inspectorate', in: McCormick, R. and Nuttall, D. L. (eds) (1982) *Curriculum Evaluation and Assessment in Educational Institutions*, Block 2, Part 3, Milton Keynes: Open University, 13–34.

Thompson, Q. and Parison, N. (1989) 'Management of Change in Education', *Public Money & Management*, Spring, 25–8.

Tinsley, D. (1987) 'YTS – Quality Assurance', *Training and Development*, 5(12), 26–7.

Walker, R. (1980) 'The Conduct of Educational Case Studies: Ethics, Theory and Procedures', in: Dockrell, W. B. and Hamilton, D. (eds) (1980) *Rethinking Educational Research*, London: Hodder & Stoughton.

217

Wilcox, B., Dunn, J., Lavercombe, S. and Burn, L. (1984) *The Preparation for Life Curriculum*, London: Croom Helm.

Wilcox, B. and Eustace, P. (1980) *Tooling up for Curriculum Review*, Windsor: NFER Nelson.

Winkley, D. (1985) *Diplomats and Detectives; LEA Advisers at Work*, London: Robert Royce.

Wolf, R. M. (1987) 'Educational Evaluation: The State of the Field', *International Journal of Education Research*, 11(1), 1–143.

INDEX